Praise for *Mercy and Melons: Praying the Alphabet*

"*Mercy and Melons* offers a practical guide and a path through the A to Z of life, beauty, and love. This reflective encounter with the alphabet makes for deep spiritual reading and invites us to take time out from the rush of life to consider and celebrate in simple words the depth and mystery of God in our lives."
—Anne Arabome, a Sister of Social Service (Los Angeles, USA)

"If you find books about prayer either too heavy or too light, you have one in hand that is just right. *Mercy and Melons* is fresh and playful, but it can hold your weight. We traipse alongside this woman who looks for the life of God in the mundane and the extraordinary, and before we know it, we have edged into profound, kind, and true connections with the Holy One. You won't be able to stop yourself from praying, even if you are in a dry spell. Pick a letter and get started."
—Melissa Wiginton, Vice President, Education Beyond the Walls at Austin Presbyterian Theological Seminary

"In Lisa Nichols Hickman's world, where prayer permeates, no, bonds the ordinary to the holy, D is for down comforters and doubt. Not devotion. Not dedication. Not doxology. Doubt. Because in a world misguided by fear, doubt is not the opposite of faith but the always honest companion that transforms. Pray the alphabet with Lisa. She helps us bring our whole and true selves, doubts and all, to the renewing journey."
—Joyce MacKichan, Minister of Education, Nassau Presbyterian Church

"*Mercy and Melons* juxtaposes theological truth and everyday epiphanies as profound questions rub elbows with keen observations of human life. Wisdom and mystery dazzle and dance on every page."
—David Gambrell, Presbyterian Church (U.S.A.) Office of Theology and Worship

"Lisa Hickman is the guide I trust on my spiritual journey. Her own passion for God whets my appetite and—in this new offering of her heart, mind, and hands—she serves food that sustains. Lisa helps me connect with God and be fed by Him. Taste and see. . . ."
—Margot Starbuck, author of *Not Who I Imagined: Surprised by a Loving God*

"Lisa Nichols Hickman is in community as she appears in print: benevolent, warm-blooded, and a keen student of the human experience. She arranges good words the way a painter might organize good colors, and in so doing presents a landscape both lovely and useful. When Lisa speaks and writes about praying, one is never quite certain if the intended conversation partner is human or divine. In the end, that ambiguity is not a problem but the gift itself— prayers that permeate every nook and cranny of this strange and wonderful God-given existence."
—Ralph Hawkins, Executive Presbyter for the Presbytery of Shenango P.C. (U.S.A.) and blogger at nextdoorpercy.blogspot.com

"I've led my congregations through praying the alphabet in pastoral prayers for several years now, and they have embraced the practice. This book will add depth and perspective to our discipline as it shows us how the very letters of our words can link the sacred and the ordinary in prayer."
—Jenny Cannon, Pastor at Bethesda United Methodist Church, Bethesda, Maryland

"As a companion for parents of newly baptized children, *Mercy and Melons* equips readers to think creatively about where God is present in their seemingly ordinary lives. We are reminded that, like the waters of baptism, God uses the ordinary in extraordinary ways. I look forward to using this resource next fall with our parents whose children are learning their ABCs, so that those parents might learn their theological ABCs as well."
—John Magnuson, Associate Pastor at Shadyside Presbyterian Church, Pittsburgh, Pennsylvania

Praying the Alphabet

Mercy & Melons

Lisa Nichols Hickman

Abingdon Press
Nashville

Mercy and Melons
Praying the Alphabet

Copyright © 2014 by Lisa Nichols Hickman

All rights reserved.

Library of Congress Cataloging-in-Publication Data has been requested.

ISBN 978-1-4267-6753-1

14 15 16 17 18 19 20 21 22 23—10 9 8 7 6 5 4 3 2 1
MANUFACTURED IN THE UNITED STATES OF AMERICA

For Leah and Caitlyn

*Thank you for the opportunity to learn the alphabet
all over again.*

God, grant me the grace of a normal day, prays my wife.

What would an alphabet of grace include?
Acrobatic, blessed, calm, dignified, ecstatic, eternal,
epiphanous, flowing, gentle, harmless, inexplicable,
joyous, keen, lissome, momentous, near, oblique,
opaque, peaceful, quiet, roomy, salvific, tireless,
unbelievable, various, xpeditious, yearning, zestful.
—Brian Doyle,
Leaping: Revelations and Epiphanies

Contents

Introduction: Praying a Jumble of Letters

From the evidence—why was I given this day?
—John O'Donohue

I remember an incredible larger-than-life statue I saw at the Cleveland Clinic. My husband was in for heart surgery. I was scared. I sat in the farthest back corner of the waiting room with the hope of keeping a quiet vigil for the eight hours he would be under anesthesia. We'd arrived at five in the morning. Surgery was at seven. By about nine, once the coffee had settled in and I knew the procedure was under way; I finally looked around and saw through the window of this waiting room a sculpture made totally out of letters of the alphabet.

The sculpture portrayed a man sitting on a large rock, grasping his arms around his knees. I've been known to pray just like that. His body was composed of every letter in the alphabet. His body, a huge jostle of words. To picture this sculpture, envision *The Thinker* by Auguste Rodin, but with the figure made of letters. The sculpture was light and porous; from every angle you could see through the letters, and from every angle the light from the windows played off the steel with whimsy and depth.

I thought of that man sitting in prayer, his body a huge tussle of letters. What word might emerge as he sits there in prayer? And then I wondered: *Is he praying the alphabet?*

Reflecting on the possibility of this new spiritual discipline, suddenly I realized the many times, already without knowing, I had prayed the alphabet.

To pray the alphabet is to let images appear from the disordered letters of our days. Praying the alphabet is naming what is absolutely most important to us when too many other voices in our world clamor for that prized spot. Perhaps our prayers stir up the letters of creation and suddenly what is aroused within us creates new touch points for our life experiences. All of a sudden the world is alive and on fire. Suddenly I understand the wisdom of the rabbis who pray, "Your word is fire."

I think of my aunt Lynn praying the alphabet at night when she wakes up from her sleep. She'll start with the letter *A*, naming friends, church friends, and family members, and continue until she falls asleep. With a new grandchild each year for the past few years, her alphabet is getting bigger and bigger.

And I remember learning in seminary that the Hebrew people of the Old Testament believed in praying through the alphabet. Many of the Psalms are acrostic: each letter of a sentence or a petition begins with the first letter of the Hebrew alphabet and continues to the last. The acrostic structure allows the prayer to be easily memorized. Suddenly, Scripture is portable. Prayer is possible in all sorts of places.

Consider Psalm 9 or 111 or 119. Psalm 111 begins with "Praise the Lord!" and then allows a half verse for each of the twenty-two Hebrew letters. Psalm 119, perhaps the most famous of the acrostic psalms, develops each letter with eight verses, resulting in the longest psalm in Scripture. *Aleph, bet, gimel, daleth* . . . continuing all the way to the last letter in the Hebrew alphabet: *taw*.

Often, praying the alphabet is an act of praise. Giving thanks for the *acorn* that turned into the mighty oak tree in your backyard, for the *bees* that produced the honey you stirred into your morning tea, for the *clap of thunder* you heard in the middle of the night and the *cupcakes* your daughter felt inspired to bake, for the *dragonfly* that sparkled across the lake.

There is also a tradition of confession connected to praying acrostically.

On Yom Kippur, the Jewish Day of Atonement, a traditional prayer called the Ashamnu offers an acrostic confession. The prayer begins: "Our God and God of our fathers, may our prayer come before you. Do not hide yourself from our supplication, for we are not so arrogant or stiff-necked as to say before you: *We are righteous and have not sinned.* But we have sinned. We are guilt laden. We have been faithless."

When I asked a rabbi friend about the prayer, he said that yes, it was structured as an acrostic prayer with twenty-four lines. The twenty-two letters of the Hebrew alphabet are each used once, and the prayer concludes with an additional two petitions using the last letter—*taw*, of the Hebrew alphabet. The twenty-four petitions match the twenty-four hours of any given day. My friend explains, "Each of us has committed every sin in the book." The confession in its very structure says we've committed every sin from *A* to *Z*.

One folktale connects the alphabet and prayer in this way:

> Late one evening a poor farmer on his way back
> from the market found himself without his prayer
> book. The wheel of his cart had come off right in the
> middle of the woods, and it distressed him that this
> day should pass without his having said his prayers.
> So this is the prayer he made: "I have done some-
> thing very foolish, Lord. I came away from home this
> morning without my prayer book, and my memory
> is such that I cannot recite a single prayer without
> it. So this is what I am going to do: I shall recite the
> alphabet five times very slowly and you, to whom
> all prayers are known, can put the letters together to
> form the prayers I can't remember."

I hear that story and I am comforted, and inspired, by the reminder that all of the letters are in God's hands, not just my own. I can keep spelling, and trying, and speaking knowing that I am upheld on jumbled days just like today.

So I center in, take a breath, and let those scrambled words settle out into a few petitions naming both the beauty and the brokenness of the day:

> *Soap. Sorry. Lavender. Lament. Honey. Help. Rubber*
> *duck. Remember.*

This is the spiritual discipline I need today: *praying the alphabet*. This practice helps me name what matters most.

This practice helps me get clear on what is most essential to name. Praying the alphabet helps me look at the evidence for why I was given this gift of a day and then to spell that out slowly and with great thanks. S-U-N-L-I-G-H-T. Praying the alphabet allows us to be thorough in our prayers because each letter conjures up something we might not otherwise have remembered: mercy, melons.

Suddenly, I can taste both.

Here on these pages, I am hoping to take that scramble of letters deep in my soul, those letters depicted on that sculpture at the Cleveland Clinic, and unscramble them just a bit. My hope is to piece together a few words and let them become prayers. In this book each letter of the alphabet calls forth two words: a word that celebrates an ordinary thing, and another word that names a holy quality about God. Then, those pairings speak to each other like that statue spoke to me at the hospital that day. This isn't quite a theological dictionary, but a practical guide to daily life as we look for beauty and hope in the things around us. I hope this kind of praying will open up your prayer life as well. Words might suddenly start to pop out in bold. You'll pay attention as one catches your eye. Let those moments become prompts for prayer.

ADVENT and AVOCADOS

ADVENT and AVOCADOS

*The alphabet's first documented use boils down to the most basic
and touching form of communication—"I was here."*
—Seth L. Sanders

I am looking at this bowl of avocados on my kitchen counter. Next to it are our girls' Advent calendars filled with little squares of chocolate, readied for the twenty-four-day countdown to Christmas. The thought of avocado and chocolate turns my stomach. But the thought of avocado and Advent, well, that transports me to my mother's kitchen.

I remember my mom in the kitchen with an avocado. And I realize, with a few toothpicks and an avocado pit, my mom taught me a bit about Advent. I don't think she meant to, but I could see as she pierced the hard shell that this was an earnest prayer. She was waiting for something to happen. After inserting a few toothpicks that radiated out the sides of the avocado pit, she'd place what looked like an unidentified flying object in a shallow dish, resting the toothpicks on top of the dish and submerging part of the pit under water. And then she would wait. Growing an avocado plant in this manner takes great patience. She'd be waiting awhile.

Wedged into my childhood window, that avocado seed, hovering over the water, supported by just a few toothpicks, helped me see there is a prayer that lingers between the pits and deeper purpose. That prayer is an Advent prayer. That prayer anticipates something new, as we boldly wait for that budding.

Advent: I know the concept, and yet I have to flip through a few paragraphs of the theological dictionary to get my bearings. Advent is a time of preparation—making room for the presence of Christ to be born into flesh like mine at Christmastime. Advent knows that something better is coming and lets the way be clear for that incision of the new. But preparation for an arrival necessitates waiting. Mary waiting for Jesus' birth. The church waiting for Jesus' return. All those schoolchildren waiting for Christmas. Indeed, three of the Advent books on my shelf have the imperative "wait" in the title. I hate waiting. That's why I love that image of my mom, in the kitchen, showing me a faithful way to wait.

The thing about waiting is that words like *alleluia* and *amen* are hard to come by when you are waiting. These two profound theological words may herald the beginning of a theological dictionary, but when you are waiting, they are all too absent. They are relegated to the end of the alphabet. Alleluia and amen mark the end of a journey, not the middle. Avocado pits are anything but the end. Alleluia and amen may be markers of arrival, but avocados and Advent are all too much about tugging, waiting, hoping, nudging, needling something different out of what you have been given.

My mom is the master of prodding meaning out of pits

and other circumstantial places where we sometimes find ourselves. When alleluias and amens are few and far between, we can do the theological work in our everyday lives of attending, accepting, leaning into awe, and perhaps even finding a place of anointing in the in-between. This is what I learned from this rudimentary greenhouse: the large seed of that pit harbored the potential for more.

The spiritual discipline of anticipating requires at least three toothpick prongs to let it hover over that life-giving water. First, acknowledgment of the broken and the blessed on this day. Second, anticipation that is not anxious, but fully aware that God will appear in ample time. Third, a wide-eyed awareness of the myriad ways that Christ breaks into the here and now. These three conditions help us anticipate faithfully, not anxiously. They help us wait prayerfully, not impatiently.

Are you waiting? I know I am. That's why I am on this alphabet quest for nouns and verbs, for the tangible and the theological: both help me understand the presence of a personal God. I'm looking for both the actual and the abstract. Augustine said it this way: some things, like the sacraments, are, according to Augustine, visible signs of an invisible reality. In the midst of what can feel like perpetual Advent, I'm looking for the palpable. And so, as the alphabet prayer begins, I am remembering that avocado pit, which keeps me rooted in my Advent prayers and helps me anticipate something new.

That's precisely why I pray the alphabet—to help me anticipate God's presence in new ways.

I begin with *A*; just as that *A* ascends up one side and

descends down the other, so does my spiritual life. Why does each day have so many highs and lows? I admire those who find their spiritual centers and seem to keep them. I'm hoping that praying the alphabet provides a bit of perspective in the midst of those fluctuations, in the midst of waiting. The letter *A* has a crossbar, the line that moves midway across the ascending and descending sides. Here is a middle ground, a place to rest; that is why I plop down on that crossbar, take a breath, check out the view, and begin to pray amid the ups and downs.

That's what my mom was doing that day in the kitchen: finding a midway point through the ups and downs of life by placing an offering of prayer in the window and letting it wait for the light. She anticipated something new would break into her day in the form of a bit of green, a sprig of budding. The great avocado experiment, waiting for those tendrils to emerge and plunge into the water, was Advent.

Years after that kitchen greenhouse, I'm living in Arizona. My dad comes to visit Tucson in the middle of August. He's been told, like all of us lured to the desert, "August will be no problem; it's a dry heat."

And yet here we sit at the kitchen table, covered in sweat after a hike through Sabino Canyon. My dad's wearing a Hawaiian shirt and pretty much looks like George Clooney in *The Descendants*. He's as cool as a, well, cucumber. I'm dripping. Even the avocado atop the salad bowl is sweating as it beads and pearls while the air conditioner lumbers to do its thing.

We make lunch and squeeze in around the table in our tiny apartment while outside a palmetto tree brushes the window. Outside, the scent of spring citrus is long gone. After sitting down, we cut into the avocado and turn the skin inside out; its rich oil is a blessed balm. We taste its delicious pulp.

All I remember from his visit is this: how much we enjoyed that avocado. And how, when we were done, we poked those toothpicks into the sides of its pit and placed it atop that shallow bowl of water, anticipating the arrival of a new thing.

Those Phoenicians might have seen an ox when they thought of the first letter in their alphabet. I see avocados. I feel Advent. Praying the alphabet, with an avocado in one hand and that deep feeling of Advent in the other, helps me to give thanks for the "one God and Father of all who is over all, through all, and in all." I see the presence of that God hovering over all, even here on my kitchen counter with the avocados, the chocolate, and that Advent calendar.

BIRDS and BE

BIRDS and BE

One of the best things to do
sometimes is simply to be.
—Fortune cookie

B might just be the most difficult letter of the alphabet. It is also an absolutely impossible word: be.

I simply write the word *be* and my whole body wants to move, cross an item off the list, get something done, send a text. Accomplish. Bake. Clean. Doodle. Evaluate. Fidget. Do something. Anything. Grasp. Heavy sigh.

Scripture takes what should be a simple action and elevates it: "*Be* still, and know that I am God"; "Let it *be* to me according to your word"; "*Be* holy, because I am holy." I'm caught here between *A* and *C* with a letter and a word that invite me not only to stay put, which is difficult enough, but also to embody a spiritual practice. I breathe in *be* with the hope of transformation, but can exhale only *do*. *Do* is in my DNA. *Be* is fleeting, like breath. How am I going to learn to "be"?

As I meditate on these alphabet prayers, I have to smile just two letters in when I get to the letter *B*. How did praying the alphabet become an awakening of the conscience?

Before I tackle the action of *b*, I settle myself with a few great B-words: *butter*, *bobsleds*, *byways*, *backbone*, *buffalo*, and *books*. I get distracted; maybe I'll make a slice of toast with butter. Or perhaps I'll go grab that book I've been wanting to read. Or maybe I'll travel down that back byway and see what produce my Amish neighbors are selling today. Or, maybe, I'll muster a little backbone and try to practice that deceptive discipline: being.

I took lessons about *be*ing from Jeanne. Jeanne battled cancer for three years. When she knew she was dying, each day she settled herself into the beauty of her back porch and watched the birds: a white-breasted nuthatch, a brown-headed cowbird, a chickadee, a golden finch, downy woodpeckers, and song sparrows. The birds calmed and comforted. There's that old children's nursery rhyme about magpies: one is for sorrow; two is for joy. I wonder if Jeanne counted her sorrows and prayed for joy as the birds graced her lawn and grazed at her feeders. As I sat with her on the porch, I was learning from her how to be still, be holy. How to let it be.

Psalm 104 begins, "Let my whole being bless the Lord!" I hope to respond to that psalm not with a frenzied blessing, but with the whole-bodied sensibility of deep being that Jeanne learned. As that psalm envisions God's grandeur, the birds are a clear part of that garb: "Overhead, the birds in the sky make their home, chirping loudly in the trees."

At her funeral, I wore a carved mother-of-pearl pendant from Jerusalem with a bird at its center. I am wishing I had told her how birds are revered in Finland. They are considered messengers from God. As they journey back and forth from the ground to the heavens, they carry messages between humanity and the divine. Perhaps I forgot to tell her because I was too busy simply being with her. Maybe this is a good thing.

Funny that it is possible to learn about being from the busyness of birds: they flit, they scatter, they rummage. But the Bible tells us to pay attention: "Look at the birds in the sky. They don't sow seed or harvest grain or gather crops into barns. Yet your heavenly Father feeds them. Aren't you worth much more than they are?"

Isn't it true that we are so scattered in our crazy doing because we worry and fret? Finnish folklore and the biblical witness invite us to listen to the divine communication those birds convey: Be still. Be holy. Let it be. Build nests in the now. Maybe when we relieve ourselves of the fret and the mad dash to do, we live into that incredible imperative to be faithfully still. I'm wondering if our doing too much is all wrapped up in our desperate attempts to instigate that divine message on our own behalf.

Be here now. The practice of this discipline—*being present, being right here*—puts to rest the tug of memories and the thoughts of the future that distract us from a full sense of *now*. Be here now; look around at the walls and the windows that surround you and be fully present. Be here now; still your life and see in that "still life" a framework for what is full and holy and beautiful.

This is a tough practice. Even my attempts to be all too often become escapes from what is here now, from what I feel now. I'll go for a walk. I'll take a drive. I'll work in the yard. And yet those motions keep me from the emotional space of my *being* right here, right now.

Jeanne taught me a bit about being. We watched the birds even in the winter snow. When I went home to my house after our visits, I had a new awareness. I saw a mother bird build her nest in the corner of our outside gutters. Would I have seen this before?

I look for nouns in the here and now, giving thanks for whatever quirky beauty they bring. I look for theological things that help me "be" better. And then I pray about actions, about verbs—does every verb take me away from this deep sense of abiding in the now? I sigh and recalibrate. I pray that a deep sense of being will fill my waking, my working, my walking.

Be here now, build nests here. Be here now, wherever you are. Be present.

This past summer our family traveled to Bird Island, tucked between Sunset Beach and the Little River Inlet. For years it was accessible only at low tide, but now that the Madd Inlet has filled in, the barrier island is accessible at all times. Clearly, Bird Island is known for its birds. Reddish egrets, black skimmers, and Wilson's plover punctuate the sunsets and salt marshes. Only two man-made structures disrupt the island: a jetty and, oddly, a mailbox. Stripped of all else, the island is an ongoing lesson in being.

Even the mailbox offers a quiet surprise: this is the Kindred Spirit Mailbox, and it may be reached only after a two-mile walk. In other words, your thoughts and all your doings have to settle out into the slow pace of your footsteps in the sand so all that is left by the time you reach this instrument of communication, all that is left for the Kindred Spirit Mailbox, are your sunburned, windswept prayers. What's beautiful about the mailbox is that the long walk is part of the prayer. Kindred spirits learn that lesson through quiet walking and through simply being amid the swooping birds. *Let go of all your doing*, I hear them cry. *Live into my way of being,* I hear God sigh.

I deposited my anxiety-driven doings into that out-of-the-way mailbox, but I am still struggling to live into *be*ing. So I am grateful for this found prayer, by poet Angela O'Donnell, in its earnest plea: "I stay here to please us, Lord, both You and me, where I unlearn to do, while I practice to be." I let these last two phrases become new wings: unlearn to do; practice to be.

COVENANT *and*
COTTONWOOD TREES

COVENANT and COTTONWOOD TREES

*When night falls, may fireflies light up your path
and chirping crickets keep you company.*
—Agbonkhianmeghe E. Orobator,
"A Prayer for a Traveler"

I have a cottonwood tree and a kind neighbor dressed in a jewel-toned sari to thank for helping me through a Thanksgiving far from home. When I think about the letter *C*, I remember my neighbor's crimson-colored sari.

My husband and I were living in the desert of Arizona: relatively newlywed, new jobs, awaiting a new child, and too far from our extended family. When I woke up that first Thanksgiving, I could hardly bear to undo the blinds and look outside. If the blinds were closed, I could imagine the last of the fall leaves drifting off our trees in the Northwest. If I opened the blinds, the first sight of a cactus would remind me all too clearly of where I was. After a deep breath I twisted the rod on the blinds, and to my surprise I looked into the near distance and saw a single tree aglow in orange and gold. I was stunned. Trees are lost amid the cacti in the desert. And who knew that out in the desert the leaves would change with the seasons? The flame of the leaves was a gift.

When my husband woke up, I asked if he might be willing to go on a pilgrimage to see the tree. He looked at my swollen belly, looked out to the distance where the tree stood, and sensed my homesick spirit. He took a deep breath and said, "Let's go."

We walked for twenty minutes, and when we finally neared the tree, we realized it stood in someone's backyard. With a sense of urgency and no mind for anyone else who might be basting their turkey, I rang the doorbell. As the door swung open, I could see the colorful embellishments of a sari. I glanced to the kind face of the stranger and asked if we might see her tree. "It's a cottonwood," she told us. "Come and see."

She led us through her home and out the back door. We stood in awe.

What is on your list of alphabet prayers for the letter *C*? First on mine is that cottonwood tree.

Here is what I came to learn about the cottonwood tree: every leaf is heartily connected to the branch by a fine but sturdy stem called a petiole. What happens when you watch the leaves on a cottonwood tree is a lyrical lesson in connected change. The leaves move rhythmically and fluidly in the wind: they just about dance. And yet the sense of deep connection is what allows this dynamic movement.

It is in the context of that deep connection that I find myself connecting the *C* of my cottonwood tree to the *C* of covenant. Connected change is really what a covenant *is*.

31

We will change. Circumstances will change. We might even argue that God appears to change, at least as we grow in our understanding over the course of our lives. All that change is hard and scary. That change could appear haphazard and uprooted. But, by the grace of covenant, we are always connected by that thin tendril. This is what allows the wind to blow and the leaves to dance. This is what allows our lives to change and yet our deep connection to God, self, and others to create a space for airy beauty.

Celia Brewer Marshall says we are "led through time and space in a dynamic relationship knows as the covenant." In other words, a covenant is connected change. I'm so grateful for her insight because *covenant* can be a slippery term. It's not a contract. It's not conditional. Yet it binds us together, with one another and with God, in a monumental way. That binding, Marshall reminds us, is never static. This covenant is dynamic and changing. Its fluidity transcends time and space. For someone who is homesick, this is good news. The stranger who opened the door that day was an integral part of a dynamic relationship. On that lonely Thanksgiving, her kindness was both comfort and covenant. She embodied the practice I am praying for here at the letter C: *Stay connected, even when change is hard.*

Praying the alphabet helps me see anew those leaves on a cottonwood tree. Together, that sense of connected change keeps those tendrils of faith intact, even when circumstances tug toward otherwise.

Some of the first words Jesus speaks in the Gospel of John are "Come and see." These words could easily be read as a tug that uproots, that disconnects the follower from all that she or he has known and loved. What the cottonwood tree and the covenant teach me is that the thread of connection is always there. "Come and see" are those lyrical leaves on the tree that dance in the wind because they are deeply connected to the root of all being, the trunk of all our faith.

Host to the homesick, Jesus beckons in the wanderer, the lost, those looking for something unnameable, unattainable, indescribable with those three simple words: *Come and see*. These three words are an invitation into that dynamic relationship across space and time. This isn't an invitation to certainty, but a summons to come and see what will unfold, what will come to be. Even as the Gospel comes to a close, the words of Jesus entice far more than they suffice: "Follow me," he says. Living into that bidding is always a process, never an arrival. A dynamic relationship is always just that: a budding consistency.

That's why I appreciate the cottonwood tree. Its rooted-ness is never questioned. These trees are majestic and solid. Like a covenant, there is no ambiguity when you are in a cottonwood tree's shade. But there is a movement to its majesty, a sense of dynamism that seeps out from under its branches. The tree is a living wind chime, nature's mobile; it is a masterpiece of dynamics and form.

I had to learn the secret to the cottonwood tree and the particular way its leaves twist and turn in the wind. The leaves rotate in this particular way because of the way the petiole attaches the blade of the leaf to the stem. I never knew this until now. I had to know more so I could under-stand just a bit about the secrets of those cottonwood trees.

When the wind blows through the leaves, the whole tree comes alive and sings. The quiet spaces are as central to its structure as its rugged trunk and leaves poised and ready to dance at any given chance.

They say Walt Disney grew up under a cottonwood tree in Marceline, Missouri. Signs at his old farm describe this tree as a place where Disney found inspiration, drew cartoons, and discovered deep beauty in the whole of nature: ants, grass, leaves, and wind. And, it is said that a cottonwood tree forms the center axis for the Lakota Sioux sun dance. Sacred from root to branch, its revered status amid the tribe demands its centrality in the sun dance. The cottonwood is a place of refreshment, inspiration, shade, and remarkable airiness. Light bounces through its leaves. Wind sings through its spaces.

We first learn about God's covenant in Genesis 9:15. There's been a flood. There's been some trouble. There has been some disappointment, even despair. God takes Noah off the ark after a long forty days adrift, and says finally here on dry land: "I will remember the covenant between me and you and every living being among all the creatures." At this point, we aren't quite sure what the covenant will be, but we are clear on two things: this is a relationship upon which we count, and this is an invitation for every living creature to come and see. Structure with spirit. Dynamics with form. Solidity with fluidity. Maybe a covenant is both harbor and sea.

Standing outside the cottonwood tree that Thanksgiving Day near the swoosh of the woman in her jewel-toned sari, I could hear in the whisper of the cottonwood tree: *Come and see*.

In that invitation, I heard a deep acknowledgment of what I have been trying to practice: *Change is hard. Let God's covenant keep you connected to Scripture, to the saints, to the Spirit that blows where it will.* The woman made that practice visible. Life is both dynamics and form. The cottonwood tree knows that. God's covenant affirms it. My alphabet prayer for covenant and cottonwood trees reminds me in a deep and abiding way to live into that invitation to "come and see."

DOWN COMFORTERS
and DOUBT

DOWN COMFORTERS and DOUBT

Your doubt can become a good quality if you train it. . . . The
day will come when, instead of being a destroyer,
it will become one of your best workers—
perhaps the most intelligent
of all the ones that are building your life.
—Rainer Maria Rilke, *Letters to a Young Poet*

I've learned the secret to what makes down comforters so perfectly snuggable and warm: their loose structure.

The loose structure of the down feathers traps air and creates an insulation from the cold. As I'm praying the alphabet, I linger on this thought and what it means for our spiritual lives: loose structures provide air, room to breathe, warmth, insulation from the cold. By doing so, this loose structure provides rest and restoration.

Down comforters, then, might just become a model for the church, for the way we shape our faith. Loose is better. Loose gives air. Anything otherwise might just be stifling and lifeless. Rigid structures stifle. Loose structures create space.

Funny that the letter *D* evokes that picture of breathable space. A straight line down the left side, a large curve around the right carves out a hollow space that traps air and provides room to breathe. Maybe *D* demands the very practice it pictures: create space. Create space for doubt without being afraid. Create space like the very feathers in a down comforter wherein the loose structure provides warmth, and rest, and sleep, and ultimately refreshment when the morning dawns.

A group of church folk in Helsinki decided to create that kind of loose structure when they envisioned the "Thomas Mass." Named for the Thomas in John's Gospel, who has been forever labeled as the one who doubts, the Thomas Mass intentionally creates a space for doubters in the pews of the sanctuary by simply giving permission, naming aloud those doubts we all feel, and offering a warm welcome to anyone who is in that mind-set. What a revolutionary thing for them to do.

Their website shares a wonderful invitation: "The St. Thomas Mass invites doubters and seekers to celebrate, worship God, serve their neighbor, and grow together. Those who feel sinful and weak in faith are especially welcome."

A few years ago, in the midst of my own doubt, I had the opportunity to visit this service of worship. I couldn't wait. What tugged at my heart and soul was so deep, I could hardly name it to a friend, let alone myself. I doubted everything.

Available to all non-Finnish worshipers is a headset for an English translation of the service. I settled into the pew and adjusted the sound level, ready for worship to begin. I sat there with the weight of doubt in my personal and professional life consuming me from the inside out. I prayed for a vessel where I could place my disbelief. And I found that vessel in the translation of the service that was playing into my ears.

Mati, the translator, narrated the service with a calming centeredness and clear, simple words. While it was the liturgist who crafted the intent and phrasing of the prayer, Mati was the one who provided the English expression. His words were quiet, clear, and disarmingly straight to the heart. As the opening prayer unfolded, I understood through him this incredibly simple yet profound petition:

> Prayer helps you listen to yourself and to God,
> who speaks in silence in the noise of every day.
> This quiet moment will give you rest. Only with
> the heart can you see well, and it helps you to see
> what is valuable in life. Just bowing down is not
> enough; where words end, God knows your heart.
>   Out of cold and dead hearts, God creates anew.
>   Let God love you.

For someone in the quicksand of doubt, these words were both rope and hope.

Why should it seem surprising when a worship service makes room for a little doubt? That's why you have to appreciate a down comforter. You know, those ones John Denver sang about in the song "Grandma's Feather Bed"?

Praying the alphabet of doubt and down comforters makes me wonder about the spiritual practice of staying loose, creating structures that aren't stifling but whose space creates room for grace and despair, love and mercy, doubt and those occasional moments of deep and abiding faith.

I try out this insight from praying the alphabet with a friend whose young adult kids have distanced themselves from the life of the church. Though they've been raised by parents who deeply believe, the adult children are now held by equally deep doubt. "Maybe you can picture a down comforter when you pray for them," I say to her. "The down comforter needs that space in between the feathers to eventually provide warmth." She tears up. I squeeze her hand.

The irony of Doubting Thomas's easy labeling through all these years of church history is that he is actually the very first person to offer a confession of faith. After seeing those scars on the side of Jesus and touching his wound, Thomas utters: "My Lord and my God!" Notice how *Lord* and *God* both end with *D. D* for *definitive*.

Mati said to me in the midst of my doubt, "Let God love you"; Jesus said to Thomas just the same. Jesus provided that loose-structure kind of space for Thomas to be real in and loved in.

Rilke wrote, "Your doubt can become a good quality if you train it. . . . The day will come when, instead of being a destroyer, it will become one of your best workers." Thomas became one of the best workers in mission as he told the story of Jesus. Christ didn't react in fear that Thomas's doubt might destroy his faith; instead, Jesus saw the one whose honesty before God would be transformed. This was a good quality, Jesus knew. Lord, help me do the same.

In my moments of doubt, and even in my moments of surest faith, I continue to be nourished by my memories of the Saint Thomas Mass, and by the Gospel's account of

41

Thomas's questions and Thomas's profession. And I find nourishment in my bedroom, in my humble bed linens. Tonight, I might just snuggle into my bed, get a good night's rest under my down comforter, and say, "My Lord and my God," even amid my doubts as I go to bed and wake up, warm and refreshed for the new day ahead.

EVERGREENS and
ETERNAL LIFE

EVERGREENS *and* ETERNAL LIFE

*Keep a green tree in your heart and
perhaps the singing bird will come.*
—Chinese proverb

My house sits on the western edge of the Westminster College campus. This is the community my husband grew up in while his father taught as a math professor. A short distance from my front door is a lovely entrance to the campus. The entrance is lined with evergreens.

My daughter and I have taken to riding our bikes there, up and down the short drive, simply because we love the feel of being embraced by evergreens. This is the place where we work on that discipline of keeping a green tree in our hearts.

That Chinese proverb, "Keep a green tree in your heart and perhaps the singing bird will come," nudges me out of my discontent. Discontent is the stuff of winter and bare branches. For me, discontent usually emerges in those "the grass is always greener" kind of thoughts that take me away from the gifts and the grace of the day and make me pine away for otherwise. Do you know that feeling? Discontent is a long bike ride with no deep breath, no singing birds, no gratitude for those evergreens.

Last fall, a few of us went up to Erie to visit a Benedictine monastery. While there, we were led in Scripture reading and prayer by one of the sisters. I resonated with the prayer on the cover of their prayer book:

> *Let not the heat of the noonday sun*
> *Wither my spirit or lay waste my hope*
> *May I be ever green*
> *A strong shoot of justice*
> *A steadfast tree of peace.*

I found myself living with those words of evergreen, praying to be a strong shoot for the just and a steadfast tree of peace.

Reading those words, I pictured that long drive up the main lane to the college in our small town where hundreds of evergreens create a canopy. Two brothers, Wendell and Dave, planted those trees years ago. Their family owned an evergreen farm, and they had the foresight to create something far-reaching, eternal perhaps. Somehow, I think that family learned how to embrace the green tree in their hearts and then offer that as a gift for others, for the birds, for beauty itself.

Hildegard of Bingen called the Holy Spirit the greening power of God. If we take her words as true, then there is no doubt that any given evergreen tree is empowered with the Holy Spirit in every branch.

Here's a place where I can really begin to pray. When I feel that sense of lifelessness, that sense of discontent, I can begin to pray that the Holy Spirit would pulse through my trunk, my branches, my needle-y places, my hopes for green. I try that on the bike ride and try to coax that green tree out from inside. Some days it works; other days, well, not so much.

When I get to that stuck place, I think of others who have lived well into similar prayers. Those who have coaxed the Holy Spirit into the barren places and found that effervescent shade of green. I think of Dave, one of those evergreen planters, and I wonder about the secret to his inner life of green. Decades after planting those evergreens, Dave was diagnosed with Parkinson's disease. I have no doubt he prayed for something greener. Visiting Dave on Sunday afternoons, I'd sit by his bed and we'd look out the window to his gardens. There his son constructed a cross made of large rocks surrounded by a backdrop of trees. Birds frequented the landscape. We'd talk. Even better, we'd laugh. Somehow the Holy Spirit seemed to seep in.

After his death, at his graveside service, on a beautiful fall day with an azure-blue sky and the crisp orange of the turning leaves, we set balloons into the air tied to our prayers and remembrances. The ritual was beautiful, but I had to laugh because I knew how many other ideas had been tossed about: We'll plant a tree. No, we'll decorate an evergreen with ornaments. No, we'll hang candy canes instead tied to prayers. Even though it was fall, having harvested evergreens all his life, his family loved Christmas. But all this was too much. Finally, we wrote simple prayers and set them aloft tied to balloons. And then something wonderful happened.

The moment we released the tight grip of our hands, God's handiwork occurred. Every single one of those balloons sent into the air drifted to the nearest pine tree and aligned in a perfect zigzag down the front. Picture a child's drawing of a Christmas tree. You would think it was a disaster, yet it was anything but. Instead, this was a Christmas tree–decorating celebration, and it was fantastic. Something about that crazy, providential tree-decorating ceremony made me know something real and true about evergreens and eternal life.

All too often we think of eternal life as something that happens *later*. The Gospel of John helps us reorient our understanding of eternal life as happening here and now. John wrote, "These things are written so that you will believe that Jesus is the Christ, God's Son, and that believing, you will have life in his name." What the author wants us to deeply hear is that "life" is eternal, abundant, hereafter; fullness of life is in the here and now.

All too often our prayers to get "greener" are rooted in what's next, what's coming, what's on the horizon. We put off to eternity the joy we could have in the here and now. Something about being evergreen is finding the Holy Spirit power now, not in a hoped-for future.

Once we realize that, then eternal life is everywhere, ever-present and effervescent. We need glimpses of that eternal life to give us hope in this life; but even more so, we need to see both bound together seamlessly in the zigzag stitch we saw on that evergreen tree.

Suffice it to say, fears keep us from eternal life now. Those everyday, subconscious, deeply rooted, rarely named fears stall us from eternal life, separate us from joy, and squelch what might be possible. "Let not the heat of the noonday sun . . . ," the nuns pray.

May I be ever green.

Ever since the graveside service on that cerulean-blue September day, I've kept a green tree in my heart—that crazy evergreen, a serendipitous Christmas tree, decorated in that zigzag glory of God's crazy work in the world.

That is God's zig and zag between eternity and you and me. Never a straight line, always back and forth; between here and there, now and then, this world and that world, the living and the dead, our hopes and our fears, heaven and this evergreen earth.

FROGS *and* FUTILITY

FROGS and FUTILITY

"Absolute futility," says the Teacher.
"Absolute futility. Everything is futile."
—Ecclesiastes 1:2

Riding my bike with a friend this week, she said, "I've been asking myself the strangest things. What is the point of it all?" To be clear, this is one of the most gracious and luminous friends I have. She is sunshine, sea breeze, and absolute grace. She's been caring for sick friends and family members, and, in the midst of changing bandages and sorting out the accumulation of stuff in basements, building up the deep sighs of thoughts and questions that are so hard to voice, let alone to answer. *Is it all futile?* I hear her sigh.

I tell her that is why we have Ecclesiastes in the Bible, and the constellation of concerns that create Scripture would not be complete without the attempts of the teacher to understand futility. This is the book that begins, "Perfectly pointless, says the Teacher, perfectly pointless. Everything is pointless." I'm not sure this gives hope to my friend, but after our breathless ride uphill, we are finally able to coast just a bit.

My Finnish grandfather was not nearly as eloquent as Qoheleth, the teacher in Ecclesiastes. Scanning through the typewritten notes he has gathered of the stories he remembered from his childhood, I come across this gem: "At Tikkipoppa's house," he writes, "the only thing that goes to waste is farts and smoke." Leave it to a Finn to so poignantly suggest that nothing in life, not one thing, is futile.

I'm praying and thinking about futility, not because I'm trying to hold on to my farts and smoke, but because I'm thinking about this usually spirited friend who feels dispirited. *Futile* comes from the Latin word *futilis* and literally means "pouring out easily." Think: leaky, unreliable, easily dismissed, poured out without end. How do you flourish when everything feels futile?

In pondering this, two faces come to mind. First, a woman I saw working at the St. Nicholas Orthodox Church in Tallinn, Estonia. Used to the constant flow of visitors, she worked without catching our eye. But she stood memorable to us, bright even against the jewel-toned icons filling the sanctuary, in her floral headscarf and vibrant flowing work clothes. She filled her bucket, mopped the floor, poured out the bucket by the back door, and then refilled to begin again with clean water in another part of the sanctuary. We were mesmerized by her steadfast work. Would the floor be in need of cleaning again tomorrow? Absolutely. Would clueless visitors trespass through her sacred halls once again? Of course. But she made futility flowery. She flourished. I remember simply the beauty and focus of her hard work, which would, of course, be dirtied within the hour.

Then I remember a young man from Guatemala working

in the tourist shop at the Mission San Xavier del Bac outside of Tucson. The salesclerk, a handsome young man with a smile brighter than the relenting heat outside, was outfitted in blue jeans and black T-shirt complemented by silver and turquoise jewelry. A large silver disk on his ring flashed as he added up my purchases.

Daily, he too greeted the tourists, sharing the incredible handicrafts of the Tohono O'odham nation—jewelry and basketry items, many of which have at their center a sacred image of I'itoi standing in the middle of a maze. We started talking as I asked him about the symbols on the crafts surrounding us. He commented, "I came to Tucson for rehab. But that's not what changed my life."

He told me that the Native American culture saved his life. He had grown up, and lost siblings, during the violence that plagued Guatemala for many years. Facing disillusionment and grief, he fled to the States. When he landed on the Indian reservation, he was struck by the wisdom of the elders, who combined the Tohono O'odham culture with the Catholicity of the mission. He learned wisdom from their tradition: *You only cry when you're born. You can't eat an elephant in one bite. You have to think like a frog: have you ever seen a frog jump backward?* My thinking had to catch up to his revelations; then I understood he was speaking about futility. Keep moving forward, he had learned from the tradition, even when faced with futility.

You have to think like a frog. I didn't even know frogs thought. I pictured my grandmother's bathroom in Oklahoma City, one that I frequented while growing up, the walls and shelves of the room covered with frogs. I wondered if she ever thought, *Think like a frog. Have you ever seen a frog jump backward?*

Two pastor friends of mine collect frogs. For Bill, the collection has come to mean one thing: *F*ully *R*ely *O*n *G*od. For those of you who needed an acronym for the letters *F-R-O-G*, now you have one. Each frog in his collection is another petition in that "age-old prayer" that comes with just a few warts. For Tom, one who knows the real effect of human sin on all of us, the collection is his differing but not cynical statement about ministry: "All ministry," Tom says, "is kissing frogs."

All of us have to face the question of futility at some point in our careers, our marriages, and our own sense of well-being. Fostering a new sense of meaning beyond that point of futility is one of the functions of adulthood. "Fully rely on God," Bill says. We do that once we've faced futility. "Kiss frogs," Tom says. We do that once we've known failure and yet keep trying. "Keep jumping forward," my friend at the mission shop says as he shares the wisdom he has learned from the elders. We do that once we've tried a step backward and realized that it is always more futile than another faithful step forward.

The young man at the mission pulled out one of the larger images of I'itoi, the man in the maze. To be clear, the symbol reveals a man standing at the dead center of a confusing maze. While he seems stuck, those who gaze on it understand that the man will not only move through this mess of a maze, but he will become a new creation in the process. It was clear as the young man shared his story that this symbol was salvific to him. I listened closely. "The man in the maze is what changed my life. I was lost in addiction. Came here for rehab. But I found hope in the maze."

The man who came to Tucson for rehab knew a few things about life's mazes. His story was a labyrinth of loss, addiction, grief, and alienation. He had every reason to want to push against his circumstances. Either he could succumb to a sense of futility, or, perhaps, he could become a new creation.

As I turned to leave the shop, the clerk said, "You know what you get when you turn the maze upside down?" I have to admit I had not looked at the image upside down. At first glance, I saw an eagle with wings flying outstretched and beak tucked down.

The image became clearer as I heard him ask, "Do you see the cross?"

Then I could see as he turned the disk upside down and thrust it before me. "Do you see it?" It took a moment, but I saw a cross with arms outstretched, surrounded by the spectrum of an overarching sunset. The man in the maze, *turned upside down,* seemed to lie on the ground marveling at the scene. He confessed, "When I saw Christ in the maze of my life, that changed everything for me."

I'll remember the young salesclerk for flipping futility around and inviting instead a new faith, an invitation to follow. *Have you ever seen a frog jump backward?* The frog knows that anything but moving forward is futile.

GRASSHOPPERS
and GLORY

GRASSHOPPERS and GLORY

The art of art, the glory of expression
and the sunshine of the light of letters is simplicity.
—Walt Whitman

Each morning, in the midst of slogging through the daily news, e-mails, and a check of the weather, I read the daily poem on the Writer's Almanac website. Living with the poem for the day has become a spiritual practice: I read the poem in the morning, and I reflect on it over the course of the day, sometimes intentionally drawing phrases or images from the poem into my conversation with God. Several Septembers ago, Mary Oliver's "The Summer Day" was the featured poem, which asks simply, "Who made the grasshopper?"

The poem begins with a series of questions that resemble those asked of God by Job: "Who put wisdom in remote places, or who gave understanding to a rooster? Who is wise enough to count the clouds, and who can tilt heaven's water containers?"

That day, as I lived with the wonder of the grasshopper in the lines of the poem, I took my daughter Caitlyn out for a walk in her stroller around the local college lake. Ten minutes into the walk, a grasshopper fluttered to the top of the stroller and gazed at me eye-to-eye. I was face-to-face with this grasshopper that had flung herself out of the grass.

For more than an hour, the grasshopper and I stared eye-to-eye as Caitlyn and I continued our walk around the lake.

The encounter was glorious.

I'll try to describe that grasshopper to you. Trapezoid lime-green face. Bulging eyeballs. Brown-toothpick antennae. And a slightly robotic smile stacked with instruments designed for appetite. Perhaps you have a picture of his face now. And you can imagine the bend of his lanky legs perched on the fabric of the stroller. But what you can't see is this: the iridescent chartreuse of his skin (do grasshoppers have skin?) that held a sheen of sheer silver pulsing with life.

I am alive, the grasshopper seemed to be saying. I am alive and so are you. We are alive together in this complicated yet barely veiled world.

Praying from *A* to *Z* is both ardent appreciation and fervent quest. I appreciate the grasshopper and give thanks to God for its glory. The grasshopper generates questions for me of God that I ask in prayer.

What do we make of this congruence? Is this God, who knew I started my day with a poem? Is this serendipitous grace, where I have eyes to see the beauty because I have been in a state of prayer? If God had the power to grace my day with a grasshopper, why isn't God up to the bigger and wider prayers of this broken world?

This is where I begin to think about glory.

Walt Whitman said there is glory in simplicity. Sunlight

shining through letters, he suggested. I can say amen to that kind of glory.

The writers of the Old Testament spoke of God's *kabod*, that is, glory, as both beautiful and weighty. So a moment like this with the grasshopper is glorious and beautiful. But there is also a surprising weight. Something palpable and real is happening here. In God's riven world, even a small grasshopper alighted on the edge of the stroller adds real weight to the day.

The last line of the hymn "Love Divine, All Loves Excelling" points to glory when it recognizes the transformation of the heaviness of glory into the lightness and beauty of God's glory with the words "changed from glory into glory / till in heaven we take our place / till we cast our crowns before thee / lost in wonder, love and praise."

As I'm praying the alphabet, I wonder, though, if the grasshopper itself has something to teach me about glory. I start to explore, and slowly I am drawn into the glorious and amazing lives of grasshoppers. Grasshoppers, they say, existed before dinosaurs. Not only can they fly, but they can catapult themselves to great lengths. Grasshoppers are able to jump two hundred times the length of their bodies. I want to watch more closely this grasshopper who is travelling with me to understand his secrets.

The *Farmer's Almanac* tells me I can count the number of times the grasshopper chirps in a fifteen-second period, add the number thirty-nine, and I will then have an accurate measure of the temperature that day. The encyclopedia reveals to me that the grasshopper has an ear on its belly, which is called a tympanum, and with this amazing ear-drum it can hear the songs of fellow grasshoppers. I wonder if that song sounds something like *Lost in wonder, love, and praise.* The grasshopper in all its glorious particularities gives me insight into God. And to think this day started out so ordinarily. Simply reading a poem.

Praying the alphabet is something like changing glory into glory. We name the real thing in our hands—that grass-hopper—and we name the real presence of God that comes along with it—glory. We hold on to mercy, we hang on to melons. We keep naming these things, as a spiritual practice, until truly we are lost in wonder, love, and praise.

When I came face-to-face with that grasshopper, I came face-to-face with the living God who creates all things for wonder, love, and praise. *I am alive,* the grasshopper is saying. *I am alive and so are you. We are alive together in this complicated world, and isn't that just glorious?*

HARMONY and HONEY

HARMONY and HONEY

We lived for honey. We swallowed a spoonful in the morning
to wake us up and one at night to put us to sleep. We took it
with every meal to calm the mind, give us stamina, and prevent
fatal disease. We swabbed ourselves in it to disinfect cuts or heal
chapped lips. It went in our baths, our skin cream, our raspberry
tea and biscuits. Nothing was safe from honey . . . honey was the
ambrosia of the gods and the shampoo of the goddesses.
—Sue Monk Kidd, *Secret Life of Bees*

My friend Emma is an expert at praying the alphabet.
Twelve years old and full of spirited energy, there
are some nights when she finds it hard to drift into
sleep. So, she prays the alphabet. I asked her which letter
she is most likely to fall asleep after and she answered,
"Ahhh, *H*."

Doesn't that make a lot of dreamtime sense? Sighhh.
Exhale. Inhale. Breathe. Ahhh-men. Even God's very
name is like a deep exhalation reverberating with the soft
sighs of *H*: Yahweh. As a friend offered once in a sermon,
if God's name is an inhale (Yah) and an exhale (Weh), then
our first breath when we are born is God's name, and our

last breath when we die is God's very name. The name Yahweh is so holy in Scripture that it was never spoken aloud back in the day. Perhaps it was just breathed.

What would you pray for at night when you arrived at the letter *H*?

I think I'd pray for honey and for harmony.

I would hone in on that line as a breath prayer and inhale and exhale the sweet smell of honey until I was asleep. I would let the deep hope of harmony swell my chest, and there in the rise and fall of breath feel that sense of peace.

The funny thing about honey is that our first thought is always about its sweetness. But I wonder if honey teaches us first and foremost about complexity. Think of the hard work in those communities of bees. Think of the many particularities of the seasons that have to be just right in order for the ground to bear flowers, for flowers to bear nectar, for the bees to collect the nectar, for the hive to create the space for nectar to transform into honey.

Honey oozes with the hard work of bees attuned to the nectar of the world around them. Honey is succulent. Honey is incredibly complex. Honey reflects a deep harmony with nature producing its unblemished best to be enjoyed with delight. The honey I most wanted to sample in my life was sold at a store in Kingsport, Tennessee, and was produced by the bees that harvested the local water lilies for their nectar. Water lily honey sounded as delightful as anything I could imagine.

Honey drips through Scripture from the first moment in Genesis when Jacob suggests to his sons that they bring to the ruler of Egypt gifts of resin, pistachio nuts, almonds, and honey. The promise God makes to the slaves in Egypt is that they will soon have a home of their own and it will be flowing with milk and honey. We meet John the Baptist, preparing the way for Christ, and he seems to have quite a taste for locusts, perhaps made palatable by dipping them into honey. And we learn that honey is such a delicious treat it should be eaten sparingly so that it can be shared with others.

Here are three things you should know about me and honey:

My friend Valerie makes the most delicious honey orange mint Southern sweet tea I have ever tasted. She should patent the recipe. Our best conversations have been on a summer day simply relaxing into the summer heat and enjoying this sweet treat.

I hate it, absolutely can't stand it, when my husband calls me "honey." And even worse, "hun." Let's just say this is usually not a moment of marital harmony. His tone in these moments always sounds more Attila and less water lily. I love it when he simply calls me "Lise."

I had a very strange transformative experience that included honey.

A few years ago I was at a writing workshop being led through a guided meditation. I closed my eyes and planted my feet on the ground, making myself stick to the process about to unfold. I placed my hands upward and open on my knees. I breathed deep and listened to the words of the speaker.

She invited us to imagine a bowl of honey being spilled atop our heads and shoulders. "Let it cover your body," she said. "Let it drip all the way down to your toes." I have to say that this was the oddest guided meditation I had ever been led through, and yet something beautiful happened. I could feel all the boundaries that normally got all too mixed up in the day slowly become more sharp and clear. There was distance between me and the world around me. I wasn't an amorphous blob of expectation and anxious connection; instead, I was wholly me for a moment. There was clarity. I felt an inner harmony and a sense of blessed separation. I didn't have to be all things for all people. I could be me, coated, anointed, loved, blessed, sweetened, and substantive.

Is this a sappy story?

Yes, but sometimes the sacred sweetens. And sometimes the sacred sets apart and makes holy. And sometimes the sacred makes everything infinitely more complex. This holy moment invited me to think more complexly about what was going on within me and to seek a deeper harmony.

I needed that moment because I had been lacking harmony in my life. All was noisy. I was noisy. If harmony is a series of chords that produces a pleasing effect, then disharmony is by definition discordant. I was there.

On the radio today, the news revealed a story of a cabin in Utah where more than sixty thousand bees had made their home in the rafters. The owner couldn't quite discern the source of the odd buzz reverberating through the house until a hive collapsed through the ceiling and into a bathroom. Certainly this gives new meaning to finding a home in the land of milk and honey. This story reminded me of how I feel when I am out of sorts. Buzzing. Discordant. Not sure of the source of the discomfort.

When I pray for inner harmony, for that retuning of my

inner life, I consider the wise words of my mother-in-law, Cinda. She spoke of that text from Romans that so many of us love but still struggle with: "We know that God works all things together for good for the ones who love God, for those who are called according to his purpose." She said, "I hear four-part harmony in those words." If you listen carefully to the buzz of bees, you might hear that four-part harmony in their tune as well.

Harmony and honey are about complexity. Is it possible to live into the invitation of these two words, as a spiritual discipline, by inviting more complexity into our lives?

Think of the four-part harmony we all love to hear: alto, soprano, tenor, and bass. Now think of the four notes this passage reveals: God works all things, together for good, for the ones who love God, for those who are called according to God's purpose. Four parts create a full chord. We miss hearing this passage when we don't remember the delicate balance, the full harmony and complexity this text intones. We are blessed by this passage when we pray for realignment in those areas where we've become noisy and out of tune.

Herein is the hope for a very simple spiritual discipline. Heat up the water for a cup of tea. Choose your favorite tea bag and pull out your jar of honey. Once the tea bag has been immersed in the hot water, stir in just a bit of that water lily honey. As the tea is cooling off, take four small tastes off that spoonful of honey. Taste one: savor the word *all*. Taste two: taste the word *good*. Taste three: sample the word *love*. Taste four: linger on the word *purpose*. Let these four words invite you from their simplicity into their deep complexity. *All. Good. Love. Purpose.* Share these words with a friend. Taste the complexity of that honey. Pray for harmony while sampling different flavors of honey.

Honey and *harmony* are the words I'm breathing when I pray the alphabet to fall asleep. They are prayers for inner transformation, that what I collect each day might not be bitter but sweet nectar, a blessing for others and a hope. They are prayers to taste the amazing complexity of each day, in all its honey, and in all its deep and resounding harmony.

IMAGINATION
and ICICLES

IMAGINATION
and ICICLES

Logic will get you from A to Z;
imagination will get you everywhere.
—Albert Einstein

Recently I came across a wonderful phrase in an essay that described ministry as "indoor exploration." The essayist, Stephanie Paulsell, said that *indoor exploration* might just be a synonym for *imagination*.

Think of the four Pevensie children in *The Chronicles of Narnia*, housed indoors for months on end during World War II, finding a dusty wardrobe and then climbing inside only to discover a whole new world.

I think of our daughter Caitlyn, who narrates all of life to her imaginary friend. We don't know her name, but we live with her presence. Caitlyn's muscles (think brain, heart, and biceps) may be slowed by Down syndrome, but her imaginary friend allows a second step in which to process and understand life. "My sister just asked me if I want to play," she will say to her imaginative friend. "She wants to play?" the friend responds. "Let's do it."

Or consider the pastor whose ordination vows include this question: "Do you promise to serve your congregation with energy, intelligence, imagination, and love?"

If indoor exploration implies going deeper and inward, rather than that natural restless response to go anywhere else "out there," then surely that kind of deep journey, that exploratory probe of the inner self, is theological work. Or perhaps, even more so, this is theological play.

One of my professors in college invited a few students to come for sweet tea in his backyard to discuss the poetry we were studying in class. Behind his home he had fashioned a lovely wooden arbor and was coaxing a few lone vines of ivy to work their way up its posts. Across the top of the beams, this professor had carved singular words into the wood: *Grace. Hope. Peace. Imagine.* Not fancy words, for sure; most of them just a single syllable. Each stood as an icon for prayer, an invitation to enter into another world for a moment and to explore indoors there the meaning and the invocation of each definition. *Imagine.* I always wondered how that word created indoor exploration in the heart of my professor from that outdoor space. What vision did *imagine* invite him into pondering? Was his work out here on the gazebo a place to pray or a place to play? Funny that, sitting there outside in those Virginia hills just a few miles away from the Blue Ridge, he could really go inside to explore those internal prayers and longings.

I love the word *imagination*. It excites something deep within me about the eternal God who created us in God's image. The God who imagined grasshoppers and graffiti art, honeydew melon and four-part harmony, pistachio ice cream and iguanas, purple jacaranda and blackberry jelly. Wouldn't it be fun to be trapped inside with God for indoor play on any given rainy or snowy day? Let's do it.

When I was growing up, Thanksgiving was always a day when I really had to rely on my imagination. Sitting down at the Thanksgiving table with the smell of turkey and my mom's sausage dressing wafting through our home, my mom would slow the meal down while our stomachs rumbled with an invitation to a prayerful reflection. "I'd like to go around the table," she would say, "and each of us say something that begins with each letter of the word T-H-A-N-K-S-G-I-V-I-N-G and say what we are thankful for this year."

My brother and I would try to plan ahead and place ourselves in seats where we would not get the letter *I*. In my mom's rules, we couldn't begin our reflection with "I am thankful for . . ." No. This invitation to prayer demanded the imagination. We needed a noun that began with the letter *I*. Hmmm, that trip to Indiana? Those icicles we always hoped to see in south Louisiana beckoning a rare snow day? I scream, you scream, we always named ice cream as that place of oh-so-deep gratitude.

As I've grown older, I've realized that Thanksgiving often asks for a different flexing of those imagination muscles. Thanksgiving all too often becomes a gathering of expectations rather than a gathering of gratitude. Expectations unmet lead to hurt. Hurt bends to insult. Insult is not an acceptable *I* answer at the Thanksgiving table.

How do we imagine new ways of being together? How does the invitation to play with our imaginations lead not to flights of fancy but to an intellectual tool, an introspective probe, an internal GPS that calls together heart, mind, and soul for something wholly new and beautiful?

Everyday theology always has something tangible in one hand and something a little more abstract in the other. If imagination is in my right hand, then I am picking up a few icicles in my left to consider how those above the Arctic Circle might use the invitation to indoor exploration as a starting point for sanity through the long winter months. The Inuit word for "icicle" is *kuhugaq*. I am glad to know this because the second most tricky letter at my mom's Thanksgiving table is the letter *K*. I've got that word in my pocket so I am ready when it's needed.

Last winter, a long stretch of Arctic cold made for a deep freeze stretching for months across western Pennsylvania. Accordingly, the icicles stretched from roof to frozen ground, and every drip from the melt of the heater only stiffened the solidity of these prisms of light and ice. Looking out into our backyard, every leafless tree and dreary landscape suddenly took on new form and color when gazed at through the surprising lens of the icicles. While not quite transparent, the icicles bent the light and the view to create new landscapes while closed indoors through the harsh winter. They became icons for imagination.

If even icicles can kindle the imagination, perhaps there is hope. I have to laugh because I'm reminded of one of those mystery puzzles people used to share on a long car ride, prior to the distractions of smartphones and iPods. The icicle always served as the ideal murder weapon, thereby leaving no trace behind but a pool of water. For those

Thanksgivings when an icicle seems like a welcome guest, I'm wondering if perhaps a robust imagination would be a better alternative. In Scripture, there are certain bounds placed on the imagination so that it does not become the work of flight or fancy. But when imagination becomes a feast of remembrance and a foretaste of things to come, God's blessing is abundant in that theological work. And so I am grateful for a theology professor who defined sin as being a failure of the imagination.

And so I go, through that gift of indoor exploration, to that day long ago in a professor's backyard to look up at his gazebo and contemplate that word: *imagine*. And then I sit again at my mom's Thanksgiving table and wonder how I might suggest that *imagining* is exactly what I am grateful for this year, icicles and all.

JUSTICE and JELL-O

JUSTICE and JELL-O

Simply because we were licked a hundred
years before we started
is no reason for us not to try to win.
—Atticus Finch in *To Kill a Mockingbird*

I'm sitting here on jury duty at the courthouse in downtown New Castle, Pennsylvania. I am thinking about justice, and, strangely, I am contemplating Jell-O.

Maybe I am thinking about Jell-O because I just went to the coolest lime Jell-O and waffle bridal shower.

Or, maybe I am thinking about Jell-O because I have been reading poetry. When I couldn't discover a good recipe to redeem lime Jell-O (though I almost settled on the Ginger Ale Jell-O Salad), I turned to a thorough study of Utah's annual Jell-O haiku contest for inspiration. Eight hundred people entered poems. Elementary school student Kira Sincock offered this winning haiku:

Explosion of taste
Vast oasis of Jell-O
Earthquake in a bowl

Krista Clement received an honorable mention for these seventeen syllables:

Limes frozen in time,
cherries suspended in sludge—
fruit apocalypse

And Louisa Keating, another elementary school student, has already come to understand this about the world:

Corrupting but fine
Jell-O is like politics
Yet never perfect

The poet William Stafford wrote, "Justice will take us millions of intricate moves." This could be the very definition of jury duty: hundreds of people renegotiate schedules and commitments, generating thousands of quiet repercussions among family and coworkers, thereby multiplying into millions of remade plans, all with the hope of justice for a single person appearing in a courtroom. Millions of intricate moves made for the sake of the one on trial with the hope of preserving what is good and just and right.

And of course, millions of intricate moves make me think of Jell-O. You know the jingle: "Watch it wiggle." If justice is fair play, then Jell-O gives a whole new dimension to that play. Is it possible that Jell-O might just help us understand justice, particularly biblical justice? This is the fun dimension of praying the alphabet.

At the Jell-O Museum in LeRoy, New York, one quickly learns that Jell-O itself began with an unjust turn. First created by Peter Cooper in 1845, the local public never quite caught on to the taste of the jiggly stuff. In 1897, Pearle Wait and his wife concocted a few fruit-flavored desserts but, then again, couldn't get others to develop a taste for the product. He sold the formula and recipes for a measly $450 to Frank Woodward, who faired a little better with the stuff but then sold the whole shebang to Sam Nico for $35. The rest is gelatinous history. But doesn't this history sound a bit unjust? And it only takes reading a few haikus with lines like the "sweet nectar of hooves" to see how unjust the history of Jell-O is for the horses.

The prophet Micah makes it sound easy: What does the Lord require of you? Do justice. Love kindness. Walk humbly with God. When we are tempted to take one step backward by positioning ourselves in rationalizing questions, the prophet offers three steps out: Justice. Kindness. Humility. Here's where Jell-O helps us. Justice is never as easy as one simple step forward. Justice, like Jell-O, consists of a million intricate moves. But perhaps even more so, justice is like Jell-O in that there is a gradual firming up over time. Micah's peers had been relying on the wrong kinds of intricate moves: burnt offerings, thousands of rams, torrents of oil. These sacrifices were all show and no real spirit. They were attempts to juggle and jostle for God's attention, blessing, and comfort, but Micah would have nothing to do with such vain attempts. Micah wanted to see solidified attempts of justice, kindness, and humility that sparkled before God.

Justice, kindness, and humility demand our all but in ·

an inward, not an outward, way. These proper sacrifices
require millions of intricate moves in our inward beings
to realign ourselves continually with what is good and just
and right and holy. And, just like nailing Jell-O to a wall,
justice, kindness, and humility—though beautiful—are all
too often fleeting. Susan Sandretto and a few colleagues,
inspired by that biblical vision for social justice, advocate
for the teaching of social justice in a public classroom set-
ting in her article "Nailing Jello to the Wall: Articulating
Conceptualizations of Social Justice."

Whether in the classroom, the church, or civic society,
clearly justice requires millions of intricate moves, and that
demands perseverance, courage, and hope. To be fair, in full
disclosure here I have to admit two things: Jell-O has been
known to make me cry with joy, and there is not one ounce
of justice in my constitution. I am a grace and mercy girl, to
a fault. And as for the Jell-O tears, my dad and I traveled
back to our Southern roots to attend a funeral. We stopped
at the Piccadilly cafeteria along the way, and there, while
walking through the dining line, we saw shining at the very
end, amid the other more high-end desserts, the sparkle of
blue Jell-O. I never knew Jell-O could be such a harbinger
of home. Maybe that's why those Utahans write those haikus
each November.

Shortly after the blinding light of the blue Jell-O on the
Piccadilly line, I found myself back in the courtroom awaiting justice. A young man from our community had gotten
into trouble at our church, so our church staff showed up at
the courthouse to support him. Our staff, drawing on those
millions of little moves, arranged our schedules to be at the

courthouse to offer our support. The judge, sensing the support this guy needed, spoke gently but with a strong edge. "Have you thought about what it means to be a neighbor?" he asked, drawing on the language of the great commandments. And then, in a stroke of gracious divine justice, he introduced the young man to the man who would become his juvenile parole officer. "This is Mr. Cross," the judge began, "and he is going to be your new best friend. You need him."

Then, in the way that only God can maneuver through those millions of intricate moves on the journey to justice, we arrived at the cross, that place where all justice is redefined and made solid. The salvation story from Genesis through Revelation and on again to that small courtroom in downtown New Castle is filled with millions of intricate moves to continually realign this crazy world toward all that is good and right and just.

Do you hear that holy haiku jingle?

This is Mr. Cross
He is going to be your new
best friend. You need him.

KIMONOS *and* KINGDOM

KIMONOS and KINGDOM

Counsel woven into the fabric of real life is wisdom.
—Walter Benjamin

With silk fabric, a few stitches, and five simple words, my grandmother gave me an incredible gift. As I am praying through the alphabet, the letter *K* offers an opportunity to pause and consider the spiritual practice of keeping the scraps and fashioning something from the remnants that is beautiful for the Kingdom.

In the summer of 1982, we sewed a kimono out of silk scraps from my grandmother's remnant box. When we made this robe, each day gleamed with the wide-open possibility. We took the day offered and relished its simple delights. My grandmother Mama Nick and I crafted it on a summer visit to her home in Oklahoma City. The summer was filled with fried green tomato sandwiches, silky red fabric, tornado warnings, and a stellar Fourth of July parade. Nights, we would hide in the basement till the sirens subsided. By day, we'd sleep late, lunch on fried green tomato sandwiches, and then pull out the sewing supplies.

My grandmother had the pattern cut for years, she told me, waiting all that time for just a moment like this. She and I talked as we streamed the material's supple drape through the needle of the sewing machine. This was our only work to be done on a summer's day. Later in the afternoon I'd swing from the tire out on the old oak tree. By evening we'd recline with my grandfather to watch Dan Rather deliver the evening's news. In the morning, we'd be back at work on the kimono.

As the silk passed through our fingertips attuned to the hum of the machine, I learned something new every day.

An appreciation for everything that could be learned in an ordinary day: that is my grandmother's secret to life. To know my grandmother is to know Southern beauty and gentility at its best. Her class and style put *l'accent aigu* in Targét before it was cool to shop there. She'd purchase a clunky men's watch for her thin wrist, and stretchy turtlenecks to wear summer or winter with her long sarong and Oklahoma cowboy boots. After shopping, we'd visit a local landmark to learn something yet undiscovered by us. "Dahling," she'd say, "isn't it wonderful to learn something new every day?"

To be clear, "wonderful" to Mama Nick is "wonnn-dah-ful." She'd continue, "This is a secret to life. You'll never die if you learn something new every day." This mantra is as memorable to me as my grandmother's ivory necklace with the spinning mandala in the middle gracing her neckline. In adolescent admonition, I dismissed this wisdom as ridiculous simplicity. Of course you'll learn every day. Of course you'll die. Everyone learns. Everyone dies. Years passed before I understood her wisdom.

Now, I know that the learning that came through the making of this kimono might have something to do with the kingdom of God.

There are moments when life loses its wonder. There are days when the routine leaves no room for learning. The familiarity of your husband, the drone of your job, even the patterns of parenting can become rote. Learning is lost to surviving. Midlife resignation overcomes adolescent wonder. Those mile markers of life no longer pass by in minutes, but in months and years, as time unfolds in diapers, laundry, and lists. Living anew every day is the realization that dying is not just about death, but also about losing the sense of wonder and possibility in each day. One morning, I woke up and put on the kimono she gave me and finally understood.

The kingdom of God is about the here and how, the near and now. The kingdom is not far away or removed or abstract nor some heavenly distant realm. The kingdom is as close as my grandmother's hand as she threads the bobbin beside me.

Certainly the kingdom is about relationships and rebirth; repentance is wrapped up in there as well. The kingdom vision claims that God is in direct communion with the cosmos. All is not chaos. Jesus used the word *kingdom* as counterpoint to empire and Roman rule. For Jesus, the Japanese fabric of my kimono would not be tinged with the lament of Hiroshima, because that violence would have found a peaceful alternative.

To see the Kingdom, to make that God fully manifest, is to find ever new ways of living.

On the back of the kimono, between my shoulder blades,

is a gift-wrapped box. Now I know, every day is a present. Every day comes wrapped in the routines and rhythms of your relationships and of your work. We become stuck in our ways. We get lost in the un-wondrous ways of the world. I had to die, just a little, inside (and go to years of therapy) to realize I wasn't yet resigned to a life without wonder.

Will today be a review of yesterday's woes, or will today allow a new discovery about my husband's compassionate spirit? Will today be a humdrum dispensation of household duties: laundry, dishes, trash, and dinner? Or will it be an opportunity to learn something new with my daughters? Will today be a race to get through the work to-do list? Or will it be an opportunity to dispose of the to-do list and to discern and learn as the dots are connected in a different way? *Learn something new every day, and you will never die.*

So each morning, after I shower, I put on my red kimono robe and get lost in its vibrant colors. Drawn into the kimono's drape are cherry blossoms and coral anemones, inky lines and intricate floral design, labyrinthine circles and leaves of sage green. Energy pulses from the scarlet dye of the fabric. The riot of color emboldens me for yet another day.

Each morning as I look over my shoulder into the mirror at the gift-wrapped box at the center of my back, I receive the gift. Each day is a present. Each day offers a moment for discovery and for deep learning. Each day is "wonnn-dah-ful" when you learn something new. Learning something new every day keeps resignation at bay. Perhaps this is what the Apostle Paul meant when he said to the Corinthians, "If anyone is in Christ, that person is part of the new creation. The old things have gone away, and look, new things have arrived!" As I open myself to the learning of *this* new day, I learn a secret to what is inside this ever-unfolding present.

To remember the present my grandmother gave me, not the kimono but the koan, I pick up my journal each night and respond to these three questions: What *new* thing did I learn today? Where did I see a transformation from the ordinary *everyday* to the extraordinary? How will I live fully tomorrow, on a *new day*?

And as I think about praying the alphabet, these three questions inform my praying: Which letter will I name? Which new thing did I see today with that letter? Which one attribute of God begins with that letter? *Kimono. Kingdom. Kudzu. Kairos. Kiwis. Kindness.*

Now, more than a dozen journals later, I look back and see a line of stitches that describe an inward journey through weariness, winsome learning, and ultimate wonder. I can thank my grandmother for the gifts of koan, kingdom, and kimono.

LOVE and LEMONS

LOVE and LEMONS

In the wintertime, in the snow country,
citrus fruit was so rare,
and if you got one,
it was better than ambrosia.
—James Earl Jones

Praying the alphabet is practice and prayer—to help us love better, deeper, and wiser. Isn't love the ultimate end of any spiritual discipline? Love is that tuck into bed at the end of a long day with tireless energy for your child or lover/mate/partner/spouse/wife. Love is the force behind the mercy of the Lord that is new every morning and helps you wake up to, once again, love.

Love can sometimes be a little too saccharine. It can get syrupy and self-serving. God's love is a bit different—it is slow to anger, compassionate, gracious, abounding in love and faithfulness. And that kind of love does not harbor anger, but fosters mercy and understanding. Still, such love can be a little tart.

So sometimes, as we practice that endless spiritual discipline of loving well, we need a bit of sugar and citrus zest to help us along the way.

Visiting friends a few years ago in California, we three young moms woke up broke and with a whole day ahead. What would we do, we wondered, and then we looked outside to the lemon tree. We plucked those lemons, brought them inside, and allowed ourselves that first sour taste of the season to pucker the lips and tongue. Then we brought out the sugar and turned on the stove to make lemon pie, lemon curd, and, of course, lemonade. We feasted on lemons that day. We turned the lemon curd into a delicious base atop a tart for other fruit to be enjoyed. Lemons became the vehicle for something else, something a little more beautiful, a little more powerful, a little more electric. They became delectable. I still remember to this day the taste of what we created with what was simply right there in the backyard.

This is the spiritual discipline I want to teach when I counsel couples who are young and "in love," parents who arrive with their children to be baptized, married couples who are strained and stressed to the point of divorce, families gathered to plan a funeral, those who are lost looking for meaning and purpose: I want them to think about those lemons that will one day be at hand. There, when resources are limited, happiness seems fleeting, and all one wants to do is take flight, it is possible in that moment to consider the spiritual discipline of stirring a bit of creative love into the lemons at hand. This spiritual discipline is about the stewardship of energy—creative love when only lemons are readily available. Recently a friend was counseling a couple whose marriage was falling apart. "How is it," she asked, "that they can be so creative in their workplaces and so uncreative in their life together?"

Drawn to Arizona in the 1800s by tales of the western gold rush, Charles Debrille Poston became the father of that state as he invested in mining explorations in the Santa Rita Mountains near Tubac. Back in those days, in this new society, Poston claimed quite a feat: "We had no law but love and no occupation but labor. No government, no taxes, no public debt, no politics." He knew there the smell of citrus under the hot, arid Arizona sun. No law but love. That would certainly turn things around. Love too easily squeezes on sentimentality instead of demanding actuality in realized practices, that transformation driven by love's electricity. Love was a requisite under that Arizona sun. There was no other choice, no other way out. Posting the banner "No law but love" would certainly change the ethos of our marriages, our workplaces, our churches.

Certainly "No law but love" is the incredible message of 1 Corinthians 13: "Love is patient, love is kind." But even our most beloved passage on love becomes too domesticated as we hear the words again and again at weddings. This isn't the kind of love you sit on the front porch and sip on a lazy summer afternoon; this is the revolutionary kind of love that sends you from the comfort of your home to the hospital or the homeless to offer a sip of something other than the ordinariness of another day. This kind of love squeezes out what the world says and ushers in the creative juice of a God who offers grace and peace and a wholly other kind of love.

Anne Morrow Lindbergh offered a meditation on love that seems a wise derivation from those words in Corinthians:

It does seem to me more and more that love has no value in itself or by itself (except perhaps first love, to the young). People talk about love as though it were something you could give, like an armful of flowers. And a lot of people give love like that—just dump it down on top of you, a useless strong-scented burden. I don't think it is anything that you can give, or if you can, it is valueless.

Love is a force in you that enables you to give other things. It is the motivating power. It enables you to give strength and power and freedom and peace to another person. It is not a result; it is a cause. It is not a product; it produces. It is a power, like money or steam or electricity. It is valueless unless you can give something else by means of it. It has taken me a long time to learn. I hope it will stay learned and that I can practice it.

If love has no value in and of itself, then it really does have something in common with lemons. Love always produces something else, Lindbergh suggested; there is always a final result beyond love.

I'm always praying for that transformation, that my love would evolve and bring gentle revolutions, maybe even some lemonade I could offer to someone who needs a refreshing drink. If we can't provide the living water that Jesus alone promises, maybe we can offer the refreshment of the lemonade that says, "I'm only human, but I am praying for transformation of all the stuff I get wrong about love."

The book of Hosea is a story about love gone wrong. Known as the prophet of doom, Hosea can seem moody and gloomy for sure. Even his children's names are a little dismal: *Lo-ruhamah* and *Lo-ammi* mean "not pitied" and "not my people." Quite a bit of pessimism to project on your infant children, but a sure sign of Hosea's frustration at the people of Israel's loving anything but God. Israel has sought other loves; God keeps wooing her back. God responds to this indiscretion with love upon love: "I will heal their faithlessness; I will love them freely." This divine promise for healing is rooted in grace and bears always the fruit of love: the lily will blossom, the vine will burst, even the green cypress tree will bud. All this because of one beautiful truth God whispers: *Because of me, you bear fruit.*

Anne Morrow Lindbergh said that love is not a product; instead, love is always producing something beyond love. This is such a helpful reminder for our disciplines of the spirit. Prayer and practice are never products. They point toward love, but maybe they ultimately lead us even beyond love toward bearing fruit.

Because of me, you bear fruit. Isn't that what this prayer suggests as well? God's love is never a product; rather, God's love is always producing and bearing fruit. If that isn't a breath prayer for turning lemons into lemonade, I'm not sure what else to pray. Breathe in: *Because of me.* Breathe out: *You bear fruit.* Breathe in: *Lemons.* Breathe out: *Lemonade.*

Now with that deep breath, as you breathed out lemonade, if there was a moment you thought that was way too cliché, then consider that motivating power of love. Make some lemon squares for your neighbor; paint a lovely lemon-shaded watercolor for someone who is ill; love freely that one person who is a lemon in your life.

MERCY and MELONS

MERCY and MELONS

I have always found that mercy bears
richer fruits than strict justice.
—Abraham Lincoln

For days here in Collegeville, Minnesota, storms have shattered the placidity of the lake and shaken the stillness of the trees. When the sun comes out, I can't wait to go for a walk. I've been reading a poem about prayer. That poem has me thinking about mercy and melons. The words are stuck in my head.

I set out for a walk. With each step around Stumpf Lake through the lengthy, sodden grass, I hear in the mush of my feet a funny mantra that emerged from the poem: *melons, mercy, melons, mercy.* A friends says this is an "earworm," when you can't get a phrase or a song out of your head. I don't know about earworms. I do know these simple words make my heart warm.

So as I walk, melons and mercy become the rhythm of my feet.

Maybe this two-step—these guiding words through the mush and muck of life, this mercy, these melons—guides our everyday prayers. This is when praying the alphabet becomes a particular way of shaping our lives, guiding our feet.

I don't always know how to pray. But I am praying for making sense of the everydayness of my life. Prayer, for me, is a notebook, a list of annotations, a compendium of solutions to living fully in life's dullest moments. Those words are waterways into the mystery of who I am and how I live my life. Prayer is both swamp and sea. Mucky and vast. Silly and serious. Full of both silt and sea life. Prayer puts into terms that name both the luminous discourse of theology as well as the lightning bug beauty of last night on the summer lawn.

Melons help me remember the ample abundance of the most simple things: dewy green refreshment, the smell of summer embodied. Mercy helps me remember the ample reach of God. "Grace removes guilt; mercy removes misery," Johann Albrecht Bengel taught long ago. These words give direction to my day: *mercy, melons.*

I need that list of annotations so I can navigate all the ways our culture calls us to tune out and, instead, be animated by something fuller, more flavorful, more ample and merciful.

Is it possible that a spiritual discipline we learn in praying the alphabet is something as simple as this: to prayerfully consider someone you know who has endured misery, pray that you might be a vehicle of God's mercy to that person in need, and then invite that person to share a slice of melon: cantaloupe, honeydew, watermelon? And so the discipline is merely to set a table, create a space, offer a slice, and say grace. If you get scared or nervous, quietly repeat to yourself: *Mercy, melons. Mercy, melons.*

Practicing this kind of spiritual discipline achieves what Anne Lamott longs for because it turns a daydream kind of thinking into a new way of imagining God, practicing faith for God, and living into a deeper spiritual discipline. Anne says:

> Imagining God can be so different from wishful thinking, if your spiritual experiences change your behavior over time. Have you become more generous, which is the ultimate healing? Or more patient, which is a close second? Did your world become bigger and juicier and more tender?

Perhaps the secret to this spiritual discipline is remembering the mercy seat described in the book of Exodus. There, as the ark of the covenant is described in all its infinite detail, the author zooms in on this particular detail of the *kaporet*. This is the "mercy seat." This is the very place where God dwells. Upon approaching the ark of the covenant, this seat of grace was the place where atonement for sins was realized. Standing before the mercy seat made one more generous, more patient, more tender.

When you set the table and slice that melon, set out a marker—even if it is just for yourself to remember—that the mercy seat of God might be present at the table as well. This, then, is the place where that cryptic beatitude, the only reflexive one in the bunch, is realized: "Happy are people who show mercy, because they will receive mercy." The giver of mercy is the receiver of mercy. Perhaps this circular logic is due to this singular fact: we are able to give mercy because we have once understood our own misery.

Sabbath was once understood as not just a day for worship, but a day to practice "works of mercy and necessity." These words are a real guidance to my otherwise all too lazy Sunday afternoons. What does it look like to bring my girls out into the world on a Sunday afternoon and aspire to practice just that: mercy and necessity? I think of Ella, who sells lemonade on Sundays and offers the proceeds to our local city rescue mission. I think of a busy family who stills themselves on Sundays by having family reading time—series of books like Narnia and Lord of the Rings—at the local senior care center. Mercy and necessity become a filter for all the other distractions and help us make wise, loving decisions about our time.

Maybe, just maybe, mercy and necessity can be realized in something as simple as mercy and melons. The abstract grace of God tasted and found to be replete with abundance.

Last week, a young musician friend named Ben from a past youth group came to stay in our home while he traveled cross-country. We watched *Adventures of Power*, a movie about air drumming. The words scrolled across the screen in closed-caption as my husband entertained other friends. The opening music began with the beautiful Latin phrase *Kyrie eleison*. A short prayer meaning "Lord, have mercy on me."

Ben jumped up and said, "That's my uncle!" His mother's brother has the Mr. Mister claim to fame. Ben picked up his phone to text his uncle in Arizona. I listened to the tune and contemplated the words across the screen.

As the words unfolded, their beauty stunned me. I had not heard their song in years:

Somewhere between the soul and soft machine
Is where I find myself again…
Kyrie eleison, down the road that I must travel
Kyrie eleison, through the darkness of the night.

We pray because we are both soul and soft machine. We need both mercy and melons to nourish and sustain us. For me, prayer is that utterance through the darkest of days and the lightest of nights. *Lord, have mercy on me.*

NAUTILUS and NOT YET

NAUTILUS and NOT YET

If nothing is dropped,
nothing will be found.
—Finnish proverb

Andrew Wyeth's painting *Chambered Nautilus* is an ethereal image of his mother-in-law painted near the end of her life. The rich and varied brown tones and textures evoke the shades of a nautilus shell. Three-fourths of the image is anchored by a four-poster bed, upon which a woman sits looking out the bedroom window amid the wispy flutter of the bed's canopy. Next to her on the bed is a basket that holds a Bible and stationery. Though close at hand, they appear undisturbed—in fact, unused. What is tangible is the palpable grief we feel from the woman sitting on the bed. She is ashen and aloof, an invalid. At the end of her bed, a chambered nautilus reveals its pearly inside. This is the place that catches our eye, for there is light here and beauty. Somehow, Wyeth has captured in the composition of this room and its inhabitant the proportion of that logarithmic spiral of the chambered nautilus.

I'm drawn into this image. I wonder what she is praying.

My hope in praying the alphabet is to learn as I go along something of the secrets in objects I might otherwise take for granted. If I stop and pause with this nautilus shell, could it teach me just a little bit about God?

They say that the buoyancy of a chambered nautilus is determined by osmosis: how much fluid is let into the inner chambers and how much is released. I'm wondering if this might be an insight for my spiritual life. What do I take in? What do I let out? How buoyant will I be in the process?

The species *Nautilus pompilius* has been a resident citizen of the oceans, remaining unchanged, for millions of years. Clearly, it has learned a secret to survival. And yet, in some ways, the chambered nautilus remains a mystery because it often resides at such a deep depth within the ocean.

When Eugene Peterson offered a fresh interpretation of Scripture through *The Message,* he wrote this of Colossians 1:27: "The mystery in a nutshell is just this: Christ is in you." I have to laugh reading these words while looking at Wyeth's painting. Couldn't we read, "The mystery in a nautilus shell is this: Christ is in you"? Could the very presence of Christ within us affect our buoyancy and resiliency?

One of the toughest concepts in Scripture is the idea that Christ and his kingdom are already present, but *not yet* fully present. Christ has come. And Christ will come again. People call this the "already, but not yet" paradox. We get a glimpse, but never enough. We get a grasp, but never a clutch. We get a bit of hope, but we keep on clamoring for more. "Not yet" is hard to live with for anyone who needs a whole lotta hope now. "Not yet" always feels incomplete. "Not yet" is what that painting of Wyeth's alludes to—the world is sometimes full of muted browns and ashen grays.

Understanding how much of the "not yet" we live in, a guy named Christopher Heuertz decided to experiment with intentional Christian community. *Let's create some chambers. Let's invite Christ in. Let's see how buoyant we can be together.* The community is named "Word Made Flesh." Heuertz talks about the grace and strength of this community in his book *Unexpected Gifts: Discovering the Way of Community*. But in order to talk about the gifts, he first has to talk about the struggles related to creating the space where grace is ultimately found. The struggles name the "not yets," those places where Christ is there already, but not fully. So in things like failure, doubt, ingratitude, incompatibility, grief, restlessness, betrayal, isolation, transitions, and the inability to know one's deep self, the community struggles, reels, grieves, and sometimes fails.

Not yet is never easy. Not yet isn't just waiting. Not yet is knowing that something absolutely necessary is not yet present. In that knowledge, there is a sadness for what is absent. Here there can be palpable pain.

With each chapter, Heuertz tells a story of an "excursion of grace" that overcomes the nagging tug of what might otherwise destroy community: radical presence overcomes restlessness; intimacy tempers incompatibility. Over time, the community learns how to regulate its buoyancy in openness to Christ at work among them. These chambers run deep. The mystery in this community is Christ. What Heuertz conveys in his chapters of reflection is something like what Wyeth put on his canvas: there are many shades of grays and browns, and yet every once in a while there is that flutter of the mother-of-pearl that beckons with beauty and allures with the deepest of grace. Is Christ the secret to that shimmery mother-of-pearl?

I've got a lot of "not yets" in my life, places where I want things to be a little different, but I can't quite get there by myself. I can say a quiet "Amen" to every chapter in Heuertz's poetic reflection. But thank God for those moments of "already." That chambered nautilus, the *Nautilus pompilius*, has learned a secret to survival that has endured for millions of years. Let a little in, then let a little out. Could this also be a very helpful secret to spiritual practice? Let Christ in; let everything else be filtered out.

Some say that Wyeth originally placed conch shells at the end of the bed but then changed to the nautilus after reading these words from a poem by Oliver Wendell Holmes:

> *Build thee more stately mansions, O my soul,*
> *As the swift seasons roll!*
> *Leave thy low-vaulted past!*
> *Let each new temple, nobler than the last,*
> *Shut thee from heaven with a dome more vast,*
> *Till thou at length art free,*
> *Leaving thine outgrown shell by life's unresting sea!*

Heuertz's community offers an invitation from a "low-vaulted past" into a new cathedral with high vaults for community by teaching a very specific practice: let some things go; let only Christ remain. Wyeth depicted a hope for spiritual growth by entering into new chambers, pearly chambers. My spiritual practice of naming loss and letting go looks to these two sages for guidance. *Not yet* can so often feel like yet another loss. But the nautilus teaches us that letting something drop might ultimately help us truly be found in Christ.

ORIGAMI and OVERCOME

ORIGAMI and OVERCOME

When you put a crease in a sheet of paper,
you are essentially changing the memory of that piece.
—Erik D. Demaine

Every morning for forty-plus years of teaching elementary school, my friend Judy would sit at her steering wheel before driving to work and pray these words, turning each line over in her head one by one: *"I have told you these things, so that in me you may have peace. In this world you will have trouble. But take heart! I have overcome the world."* With these words, she prayed for her own troubles and for strength to overcome them in order to love and encourage the children in her classroom. But even more so, she prayed these words to lift up both the known and the unknown troubles of each child in her class. These words, for years, were her daily prayer. I love her for this. In church, when we sing the praise song by Brian Doerksen titled "You Shine," which draws on the beauty of this verse in the chorus: *"In this world you will have trouble."* The lyrics *are* the biblical text. I look at Judy and give thanks that these words have flesh and a story to give witness to their deep truth. We overcome together.

In some ways, Judy was praying the alphabet as she remembered each child by name and graced them with those words from the Gospel of John in prayer. As she folded her hands in prayer, she named each child and prayed for their deep and abiding sense of peace that they could overcome any struggle they faced in their day.

Overcome is such a profound word, I tread lightly here. Overcome is as large as a people finding liberation from oppression. Overcome is as intimate as a person finding liberation from a thought pattern, a habit, an addiction. Overcome is about those hurdles in life. But even more so, overcoming is about forging new memories from past oppression.

As noted in the chapter opening epigraph, Erik Demaine says, "When you put a crease in a sheet of paper, you are essentially changing the memory of that piece." In thinking about prayer, I'm also thinking about origami and wondering if prayer is something just like paper folding; in the folding and unfolding of words and sighs in prayer before God, I wonder if we are changing our memories, changing the essence in some way of the pieces before us.

My friend Jason practices this act of folding as a spiritual discipline. Every morning he folds three paper cranes. He is aiming for three paper cranes for 365 days, minus a sabbath here and there, toward that blessed one thousand. But the number isn't the outcome that matters in his origami practice; what matters are the people and the petitions they stir as he folds. "This morning," he once said, "I prayed for my wife. I made three folds, each time praying her name—Shannon. And then I simply had to stop and pause."

I begin wondering what Scripture verse I would pray while doing origami. I would fold and pray, fold and pray. I would pray to overcome those things that hold me back from God's will. Then I knew in an instant: "We have access by faith into this grace in which we stand through him, and we boast in the hope of God's glory. But not only that! We even take pride in our problems, because we know that trouble produces endurance, endurance produces character, and character produces hope. This hope doesn't put us to shame." I reduce the passage to key words to call each line to mind: *access, grace, boast, glory, pride, trouble, endurance, character*, and *hope*. These nine words become nine folds, and as I silently pray them to myself, I imagine folding a line with the first sentence as I take one corner of the square across the page to meet the other corner. If overcoming is about creating new memories, then Scripture is precisely what I want etched into my neural patterns.

It is possible to make an origami envelope in just nine folds. With each line of a fold, I picture a line of the Scripture written across the dashed edge. Even daydreaming about this practice, this way of praying, gives me peace. Is it possible that even with these folds, I am changing my memory? I finish the envelope and mentally tuck my prayers inside.

I think of Judy, sitting in her driveway, making paper envelopes to tuck her prayers into. Prayer is certainly a practice that aims to overcome. But sometimes we need new ways of considering our practices of prayer, new methods to create new memories. I keep thinking about this origami kind of prayer, and I wonder what kind of insert I could put into the bulletin to teach the practice of folding that would contain all the steps but also enfold each line of Scripture, so that each fold became a way to pray. *Trouble produces endurance; endurance produces character; character produces hope.*

At a church breakfast one morning, I asked Marite about her son Sean's recent wedding. The two families, one from Japan and one Cuban-American, met in Florida to enjoy a week of wedding celebrations. To communicate, they hired a translator.

At the celebration, Marite's brother-in-law shared through the translator about his battle to overcome cancer. "He never talks about this," Marite told me. But the translator, strangely, provided a space. Miki's mother listened quietly to his story. Soon, she started folding paper cranes. This needed no translation. She folded and folded, then folded some more. Sean started to fold, so did Miki. Sean's best man, Barry, started to fold. Sean and Barry had learned to fold origami in school under the instruction of an insightful teacher who knew them well. Years later, they're folding cranes in crisis. Soon, there were a thousand cranes.

Several nights before the wedding, Miki's mother asked to stay home from a pre-wedding gathering. When the party returned to the hotel, her task was complete. She had strung the paper chains to create an origami mobile. They were a gift, a prayer, to help overcome cancer. She gave them to the brother-in-law.

When sighs are too deep for words, when troubles are too hard to name, I wonder if folding offers a way into the pain.

109

There, folding offers a place for transformative change. I understand, deep in my bones, how this folding might change a person. I think of my friend Marite and see how this folding might even change a family system. But then I read an amazing headline, and I wonder if it is possible that such folding might even change a nation.

On December 5, 2004, Kylie Morris, of the Bangkok office of the BBC News, reported that "the Thai government has dropped an estimated one hundred million paper origami birds in an unusual peace bid." Could folding change the memory of a nation?

When violence and misunderstanding erupted between the North and the Muslim South, Prime Minister Thaksin Shinawatra creased together a plan: start folding. More than one million origami cranes were made, all with prayers and hopes written inside. Each crane contained a name; even the prime minister himself signed off. Then a peace plane dropped the cranes over the provinces of Narathiwat, Yala, and Pattani. Can you imagine the thrill of standing under the flurry underneath?

I contemplated sharing this story in my "Peacemaking and Just War" class, but for some reason I didn't think words would do the story justice. Instead, I closed my eyes and started piecing together prayers while folding: *In this world you will have trouble. But take heart! I have overcome the world.*

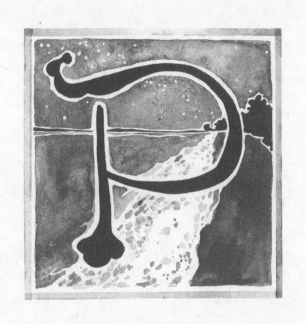

PRAYER and the
PHOSPHORESCENT BAY

PRAYER and the PHOSPHORESCENT BAY

Prayer . . .
The soul in paraphrase, heart in pilgrimage.
—George Herbert, "Prayer"

Praying the alphabet is about a particular way of paying attention and then joining two hands in prayer.

In one hand, a tangible object: peach, Play-Doh, petunia, pansy, peanut butter, porcupine, or a prickly pear cactus. (All right, maybe we won't literally pick up in our hands those last two. We'll leave the porcupine and the prickly pear cactus as objects of contemplation.)

In the other hand, we try to grasp the intangible—those things of faith, those attributes of God, those spiritual gifts we long to receive: providence, patience, perseverance, peace, praise, penitence, prevenient grace, petitions of prayer. And then, with two hands interlocked in prayer, we draw these disparate things together: peaches and providence, Play-Doh and patience, petunias and perseverance. We let the two speak to each other, and then to us. We let God speak through them so that we might hear a whisper of provision for the living of our days. Our meditation is grounded by what is before us: peanut butter. And then lifted by what we long for: peace.

It's prayer that comes to mind, though, first and foremost, when I pray for *P*. Prayer is the foundation to all other words. Prayer is that deep well where our souls rise up with the hope of meeting that powerful God. *P* also brings to mind the most amazing place I have ever seen, the Phosphorescent Bay, but first I have to tell you about a musician we met.

I met a man in New Orleans—a jazz trombonist—who lived in Musicians' Village, a Habitat-built community filled with rainbow-colored homes: an arc of hope after the flood. We knocked on his door one morning as our work crew helped in the area. He was eating his grits and saying his morning prayers. He exuded the Louisiana axiom that a man full of grits is a man full of peace. I couldn't stop thinking about his earnest and ordinary, and yet so holy, start to his days. He prayed his rosary. He cooked his grits and tasted peace.

I have never tasted a prayer, nor have I ever said my grits. Something about breakfast there with this man full of jazz lifted both to my tongue, showering the day with meal.

"Prayer is not a lever we use to nudge God in a specific direction." These words in an editorial by John Buchanan in the *Christian Century* stirred a response from Walter Brueggemann. In a letter to the editor, Brueggemann disagreed: "Prayer," he wrote, is a "primitive engagement that violates our best reasonableness. . . . It is a genuine engagement between two lively partners." For this Old

Testament scholar, that lively engagement between two partners might nudge just one of those partners, God, in a different direction. Does prayer have the power to affect God? Does prayer transform situations? Does prayer change us or God?

What *is* prayer?

The dialogue between the scholar and the pastor above took on particular meaning in my prayer life when we discovered that our second daughter would be born with Down syndrome. While my prayers ranged from discordant "whys" to heavy sighs, there were many times I simply had not one word for prayer. One night I found myself sitting on the bathroom floor, in tears. Trying to turn to God, I began praying the Lord's Prayer, but I couldn't get past "thy will be done" without sobbing. At this point I wasn't considering theological issues; I simply longed for God.

But the question of whether or not prayer is a lever we use to nudge God was raised for me one Sunday morning at church when a sister in Christ wheeled up to me after I finished preaching one Sunday morning and stretched out her arms to my protruding belly. "Let me pray for those X and Y chromosomes," she told me. I didn't have the heart to tell her that X and Y chromosomes do not cause Down syndrome. Even though I was surprised by her offer, her request was so fervent and her manner so earnest, I couldn't bear to say no. Even more so, Rose's prayer life was lively—a lifeline for many.

As she prayed, my brain began to spin. Is this the prayer God wants from us? Would a prayer like this have the power to change God's creation? Is Rose being too bold, or is she boldly showing faith and trust? Would this prayer come true if I let myself really believe the possibility of a different outcome?

We collapse into prayer knowing that in this place of transformation grief is halved, joy is doubled. For those moments when prayer is a falling backward, we rest assured that it is God's prevenient grace that catches us. For those moments when prayer is stepping forward in faith, we give thanks for the perseverance that spans the chasm of doubt.

What I do know about prayer is that it is a cloak of consolation, a garment of praise, a comfort for those who grieve. I think of Peter praying in south Louisiana. I think of Brueggemann praying through the prophetic voice of the Old Testament. I think of Rose praying for me and our daughter yet to be. I think of Margaret, my aunt Lynn, Emma—all women of great spirit, who faithfully pray the alphabet each morning and night.

Recalling the depth of these prayers, I am reminded of the deep and most beautiful place on earth I have ever visited: the Phosphorescent Bay in the southwest corner of Puerto Rico, in a small village named La Parguera. On a moonless night at midnight, visitors are invited to take a boat ride out into the middle of a dark and deep bioluminescent bay for a swim. There, amid the roots of the mangrove trees, millions of microscopic organisms sparkle in the sea water when stirred by the energy of your body's movement. The effect is something like swimming in the stars. Your body drips with light. Truly, this is a cloak of majesty, a garment of praise as the creatures produce light upon light, seen all the more on the darkest of nights.

Maybe prayer is most like this. We jump into the swamp at midnight with the hope of meeting an energy greater than our own. We are lost in the dark, but we leap with faith. And there we are met with light beyond our imaginations. We are met with a grace that we draw around our shoulders as a garment for our grief, a cloak to console, a comforter that holds us together. As we move, tentative at first, we suddenly see that we are swimming in the stars. We are cloaked in a surprising light. Our prayers aren't lost in the deep, but lifted into an odd but beautiful luminosity.

QUESTIONS and
QUEEN ANNE'S LACE

QUESTIONS *and*
QUEEN ANNE'S LACE

Christ indeed answers our questions;
but he also questions our answers.
—Rowan Williams

There is an urban myth, even in our two-stoplight town, that goes like this: a woman at our local senior living center keeps a paper bag on her kitchen table. Every time she has a question for God, she writes it on a scrap of paper and throws it into the bag. "When I die," the urban myth quotes her as saying, "bury me with my questions. I'll bring them straight to God."

I like this story. I wonder what questions she might have written, and what questions I would add to her growing pile. Maybe she, too, was praying the alphabet, an alphabetic list of questions she had neatly ordered and readied to present to God when necessary. Praying the alphabet is just this kind of quest.

Sometimes the questions are grand and existential: Why do people suffer at the end of life? Why do evildoers seem to prosper? And sometimes the questions are humbler. Now, as spring unfolds around me, one of those simpler questions comes to me: Why *did* God make weeds?

Perhaps if you've had your knees in the dirt, this might be one of your questions as well. Don't get me wrong, there are some beautiful weeds: the purple loosestrife, the dame's rocket, the oxeye daisy, the star-of-Bethlehem, and even the water lily are all weeds. Goldenrod, thistle, and jimsonweed are all slightly more beautiful than their weedy categorization. And then, of course, there is Queen Anne's lace.

At the Amish farm just up the road from me in my two-stoplight town, the front lawn is mowed on either side of the walk winding up to the sky-blue door on the straightforward white clapboard house. What happens, though, after the mowing, is that a winding path of weeds remains alongside the walkway and the drive after the grass has been cut. These weeds are Queen Anne's lace. They soften and grace the path.

Is it possible that our questions, those persistent weeds left standing after so much has been mowed down, might just form a graceful path to the living God?

In this time of Google algorithms, we have the possibility of categorizing our questions in a way unlike any other of the past. Jennifer Daniel explores these questions in her book *Googlepoetics*, and suddenly a list of everyday, ordinary questions are seen in a new and intricate way. We type in the word *Why*, and slowly there emerges a list of questions on people's minds:

Why is the sky blue
Why did the pope resign

Why do men cheat
Why did I get married?

Why doesn't she like me
Why doesn't he like me?

Why don't oil and water mix?

My husband says that questions are easy. What is more difficult, he argues, is constructing a system of belief. Something that holds together. Cynics simply ask the opposite. But a creed expresses some belief despite the persistence of questions. "I believe; help my unbelief," is anything but cynical. This is a confession of faith, nevertheless.

I think about my garden outside and my inherent lack of gardening skills. I try to let my husband's philosophy encourage me here. *Weeds are easy to pull,* I tell myself. *The difficult work is constructing the garden.*

A few of my friends are trying to construct a different kind of garden, a Christian community, in Northumbria, England. They work together, play together, cook together, eat together. They pray together, and, yes, they weed together. Every day, in the rhythms of this community, they ask themselves three questions beginning with self, then continuing with two questions for the community:

Who is it that you seek?
When we find ourselves in a strange land, how then shall
we live?
How shall we sing the Lord's song in that strange land?

They learn to live, breathe, pray, and weed their responses to these questions. The answers they discover are not always word or creed, but more often than not a whisper, or even a weed. Beauty, strange beauty, catches their eye. Some things are mowed down, and what remains is lacy, elegant, aloof, yet full of grace. They discover that winding path, highlighted by the weeds, narrated by questions, and always a gracious space.

That's the path Job finally found. He lost his wife, his children, his job, his livelihood. The question the book asks is this: When all else was mowed down, would Job lose his faith in God? The answers his trio of friends suggest are so banal and bland and cliché that one might think he would well lose his faith in God, but by chapter 38, Job still stands in the presence of God only to hear a long list of questions:

> *Where were you when I laid the earth's foundations?*
> *Tell me if you know.*
> *Who set its measurements? Surely you know.*
> *Who stretched a measuring tape on it?*

Those three questions are just the beginning of God's bag of questions for Job. Suddenly the tables are turned and our long list of questions is drenched in the ocean, thrown to the stars, trampled by the bear, and scattered by the four winds, all of which were created by God's power, which we can never understand or question. Here in these verses in chapter 38 are at least thirty questions asked by God of Job.

Why weeds? we ask God. Perhaps the answer comes to us through the words of Ralph Waldo Emerson, who stated that a weed is "a plant whose virtues have not yet been discovered."

As I go about the work of praying the alphabet, my hope is to somehow be a quotidian theologian. That is, to go about the everyday theology of our ordinary lives by looking at those weeds and finding in them something that is no longer problematic, and instead provides, perhaps, a quest for zest.

Kathleen Norris did a little of this work in her book *The Quotidian Mysteries*. Instead of garden weeds, she is considering the ubiquitous pile of dirty clothes: ever-present, always annoying. If she can find an answer to the question "How can laundry become liturgy?" then perhaps she might draw a little closer to God. I'm asking: How do weeds become creeds? That is, how do we believe in something we would otherwise consider disruptive?

Queen Anne's lace attracts some amazing visitors: the swallowtail butterfly, the honeybees and bumblebees, the viceroy butterfly. And Queen Anne's lace creates a cooler microclimate that allows other plants to flourish when inter-cropped with it. This is the stuff that is helpful to know; it is also good to know that it is easy to confuse Queen Anne's lace with poison hemlock, so look carefully for the red drop in the center that looks like blood and shows a little prick from Queen Anne herself.

Learning this, I know just a bit about how a weed might become a creed. The creed might still be filled with questions, just like the intricate lace of those weeds, but somehow the belief, when leaned into, draws forth what flutters and prospers, what graces and alights. Is it possible that a creed is a confession whose virtues have not yet been discovered?

Maybe the spiritual discipline the letter *Q* reveals is this: asking, as we pray the alphabet, for illumination while we pay attention to what we otherwise might all too easily toss aside as unimportant, uninteresting, unreasonable. And then, seeing at its center—whatever "it" is—that prick of blood, that illumination of Christ, that remnant of the divine at its very core.

When we master that discipline, then when we ask, "Why is the sky blue?" or "Why did I get married?," we'll see at the center of each question the very presence of Christ.

RAINBOWS *and*
RESURRECTION

RAINBOWS and RESURRECTION

My heart leaps up when I
behold a rainbow in the sky.
—William Wordsworth

My grandmother Mama Nick sent me these words shortly after the devastating tornadoes in Moore, Oklahoma. Mama Nick lives an hour north. She spent several evenings in the basement this summer sheltered from the storm. In her note to me, written by her hand humbled by Parkinson's, she adds: "and so do I."

I can only imagine the deep breath of relief a rainbow in the sky might mean to those who emerge from their basements after such terrifying weather. Hearts leap, absolutely, with pure relief. But I wonder if Wordsworth had our response to rainbows quite right. I wonder if a rainbow tugs on *every* point of our bodies, encouraging a full-bodied response to that beauty in the sky.

My heart leaps. Rainbows, absolutely, make that liveliness possible. But it is resurrection that makes us alive. One definition for resurrection may be as simple as this: literally, "standing up again life."

As I am praying the alphabet here, I am careful when it comes to what can seem to be clichés in words like *rainbows*, and maybe even *resurrection*. Some words are too loaded with easy joy to prayerfully unpack. But my rainbow prayer runs deep. In the Hindu tradition, the chakra system lays out a vital point of energy at seven different locations in the human body. Each of these seven centers tugs on a particular life force, and each one is represented by a color: red, orange, yellow, green, blue, indigo, and violet. Watch out, Roy G. Biv.

Is it possible that when a rainbow appeared to Noah in the sky after the devastating weather event he endured, the covenantal promise was so vitally important that God wanted to ensure Noah would not easily forget? And so this amazing rainbow didn't just tug on the corners of Noah's heart as it offered hope and promise. Instead, God tugged on every vital center of Noah's body—in that Roy G. Biv kind of way—by making sure that every color in the sky drew on the deepest energy at each point in his weary body. This was a full-bodied promise God revealed to Noah. This full-bodied promise helped him stand up again, tall and strong. As the rainbow's light tugged on each part of his body, this promise would not be easily forgotten, or so hoped the Lord God.

Now, when I look at the arc of that rainbow in the sky, I see a full-bodied promise that redeems the rain that proved so destructive by coloring the sky through those prisms of light.

I have a friend who doodles in the margins of her Bible. Her Bible is a riot of color and joy. Each text bursts with color, doodles, prayers, and even rainbows.

Her color-filled Bible creates inward peace and outward joy. As I saw those rainbows burst forth on the page, I wondered if these pictures might be little reminders of that full-bodied promise, if those colors on the page might tug on the energy centers in her body, providing a lift and offering hope.

That tugging on the energy centers throughout our bodies may just be a bit of what helps us live into that "standing up again" resurrected life. The Holy Spirit renews us in our weary places, our dead places. and draws forth a riotous energy. We find that energy as we dwell with Scripture and let it tug on us.

One morning I thought I'd burst out the highlighters and try doodling in my own wide margins. I turned to Colossians 3 and started reading at verse 12:

> As God's choice, holy and loved, put on compassion, kindness, humility, gentleness, and patience. Be toler- ant with each other and, if someone has a complaint against anyone, forgive each other. As the Lord for- gave you, so also forgive each other. And over all these things put on love, which is the perfect bond of unity.

Next to the text I wrote, "seven items to put on each day beginning with compassion and ending with love." As I thought of those seven items, I wanted to imprint them in my memory, so I sketched seven arcing lines from those words to the corner of the page. Without trying, I had created a rainbow.

Over the seven lines I wrote the items to wear: compassion, kindness, humility, gentleness, patience, tolerance, and, ultimately—love.

I couldn't resist and simply had to pull out the highlighters; I marked lines of neon red, orange, yellow, green, blue, and purple. Suddenly, rainbows filled the page.

Then, as I journeyed through the day, I tried not just to "think about it," but to "live with it." This is the beauty of Colossians 3:12-14. Listening with the eyes filled the page with rainbows. Reading between the lines opened up a riot of color. The day turned just a bit brighter. I found some new energy. I gained the ability to stand up again and face the day in a Christ-centered way.

On my office bulletin board I have a quote from a Christmas card written by the president of Villa Maria, a spiritual home for the Sisters of the Humility of Mary in New Bedford, Pennsylvania. He wrote:

> *In the Christ child, God became physical. . . .*
> *On behalf of our community, I pray that you will*
> *Discover anew the presence of God in*
> *physical exchanges of affection*
> *That are only possible because Christ*
> *embraced humanity.*

Could it be that both rainbows and resurrection are first and foremost physical? That they tug us out of the tomb and place us before the community to offer that physical exchange of affection and peace and joy to others?

Maybe this is resurrection: God's vibrant and amazing Word tugs on the tired flesh of our bodies. Spirit and flesh are never disconnected, but always intimately connected. We listen with our eyes. We sing with our flesh. We see with our hearts. That full-bodied tug makes these old bones live in spirited and vibrant new ways. My whole body leaps when I see a rainbow in the sky. My whole body is tugged into resurrection life and given a full-bodied promise that I will never forget because it is there in my bones, and in my blood, and in my very breath.

Here, the colors of Roy G. Biv meet the virtues of Colossians 3:12-14: compassion is red, kindness is orange, humility is yellow, gentleness is green, patience is blue, tolerance is indigo, and love is that amazing shade of violet. I can't wait to bring these colors to life, to a new and re-deemed, resurrected life.

SOAP and SANCTIFICATION

SOAP and SANCTIFICATION

The cure for anything is salt water:
sweat, tears, or the sea.
—Isak Dinesen

Give me salt water any day—sweat, the sea, maybe even tears—nothing cleanses quite as thoroughly. Or so I thought, until the day I made soap and learned a little about sanctification in the process.

Sanctification is a mouthful of a theological word. As a Southerner, I am more comfortable with the five-syllable drawl of "Y'all" than the starchy sound of a word drawn from the fifteenth-century Latin *sanctificationem*. I hear *sanctificationem* and all I can understand is "sandy vacation," and I definitely could use one of those.

But sanctification has a lot to do with everyday theology. Here is a word that gives me pause as I'm praying the alphabet. Sanctification is the way that all of us in need of flip-flops and a long walk in the sand are made holy—not by the relaxation of an escapist vacation, but by the work of the Spirit within us making us new in our everyday lives. That kind of transformation, our culture would tell us, is possible only with Dr. Oz, Oprah, and Joel Osteen as our life coaches. But the work of the Spirit in sanctification surprises us. We sense that transformation in worship. We lean into that transformation through ethical choices. And we hope in that transformation to be fully realized, because we get a foretaste of that holiness in our crazy here and now. Sanctification is part ethic, part expectation, and a whole lot of effort by the triune God to draw us into an essential relationship with a holiness greater than any given holy grail we casually toss around.

Maybe that's why we long for those sandy vacations. We hear one thing from our culture and another from Scripture. Our efforts go into untangling the messages instead of leaning into that holiness, the sanctifying work of the Spirit that offers something new.

Lent is a season that reminds us of what it means to lean into that holiness. We sacrifice something as a Lenten discipline to understand the sacrifice of Christ. We soap up and get clean to be Easter Sunday–ready. We sense that there is something greater than Peeps and March Madness and even those spring azaleas.

"*Laissez les bons temps rouler*" (Let the good times roll) always preceded Lent in south Louisiana. As a girl growing up in Baton Rouge, I knew more about Mardi Gras beads and the parade routes of New Orleans than Jesus' journey to Jerusalem. My parents would pack two ladders, one long board, and two children in the car and drive south to New Orleans for Fat Tuesday, the pinnacle day in a weeklong Mardi Gras celebration.

After reaching St. Charles Avenue, my dad would set up

the ladders with the board stretching across the top to allow my brother and me to sit there for the best view. There we would scream, "Throw me something, mister!" and we'd wait for our hands to be filled with beads, doubloons, and candy.

But even then—when I was more interested in quick prayers to Saint Expedite at Our Lady of Guadalupe Chapel in the French Quarter than in a long and ponderous Lenten penitence—something about those Mardi Gras days left me eager to return home and scrub down with soap and water as quickly as possible. Perhaps those suds marked a more appropriate entrance into the weeks of Lent than I ever realized.

One Ash Wednesday, I learned how to make soap with a friend. You measure the lye, heat the oil, and, at the right temperature, bring them together and stir slowly. The chemical process—called "saponification"—is dangerous, requiring gloves and safety glasses. Nothing like adding another syllable to make these words really confusing. But I wonder if saponification, that act of making soap, helps us understand a little bit more about sanctification.

What we realized in the midst of making soap—a cleansing agent—was how appropriate it was to be doing this on Ash Wednesday. From the ashes of Wednesday to the oils of Easter morning, Lent is bathed in these elements. Together, ashes and oil create a cleansing agent that is something like the work of sanctification in our lives.

Lye is formed when water passes through ash. Ashes yield lye. Stirring those ashes reminded me of everyone in our congregation who had experienced loss and grieved over the past year, experiencing in a painful way what it means for us to be creatures of the earth, "from ashes to ashes, dust to dust." Somehow all the losses in church and community and the circle of my family came to mind in that lye.

But alongside the dust there was the oil, the lubricating fluid of grace and extravagant love—the selfless expressions of gratitude and service lived out among our congregation members each and every day. An untimely death being transformed by resources donated to build a preschool. Widows preparing meals each month because our town is beyond the reach of meals-on-wheels deliveries. Youth finding ways to make a difference through creative service.

Ashes and oil measure the most important season in which we journey. From the ashes of Ash Wednesday to the oil poured out by the women at the tomb ready to anoint Jesus in his death, from the dust of the trail marking the way to Jerusalem to the spices and oil intended for a body laid to rest in a tomb, ashes and oil frame our resurrected reference to renewed life.

When combined, the cleansing agent that ashes and oil create is evidenced in Jesus Christ. He is the soapy Savior who forgives us, cleanses us, calls us, re-creates us, marks us, and directs us in our worship and discipleship. His ashes mark a love that, in its dust, is the deepest of human frailties. His oil of anointment, intended for us, marks a love that is extravagant and costly, unconditional and everlasting. It won't rub off.

Last year our church hosted an Easter event for friends from the local rescue mission. There I met Mike, a middle-aged man whose life is full of the ashes of addiction and the grace-filled oil of redemption.

Each night before the doors of the mission are shut, Mike goes outside. This week he was doing just that when a state trooper pulled up beside him and asked if everything was all right.

"All right?" Mike said. "I'm fine. Why?"

"Because I can see that you are talking with someone— and yet there is nobody around," the trooper said.

Mike nodded, pointed up, and said, "I'm talking with him."

Mike knows too much about ashes. He's just now learning about oil. That oil is poured out anew each night as Mike stands on the street under the stars and talks with God. The journey between ashes and oil has been one of penitence and one of salvation. For so long, Mike prayed those Saint Expedite prayers for a quick fix. Now Mike knows the penitential truth: the journey isn't flashy or easy. Becoming a new creation is marked by the shedding of dirt, the cleansing of filth, and the scrubbing away of grime. That journey from soil to soul requires the naming of ashes and the claiming of oil. This isn't just soap; this is sanctification.

The season of Lent is marked by ashes and oil, and from it emerges the extravagant surprise of Easter. No longer do I need two ladders with a bridge of wood across the top to secure the best place for the parade. Instead, I have two other markers that bridge the journey: ashes and oil. Even more so, through that journey I am bathed and cleansed by Jesus the Christ.

This Ash Wednesday, as penitents leave our service of worship, what I want to place in their hands is a small bar of soap labeled with a prayer like this:

Lent begins with ashes, the ashes of last year's palms sealed onto our foreheads; they mark a prayer for the journey ahead.

Easter arrives with oil, as the women who arrive at the tomb with oil and spices are stunned to find their Savior alive.

Soap is made from ashes and oil. With it we are cleansed, refreshed, renewed. The journey to the cross offers that same opportunity to come clean.

May this soap be a reminder of that process, for all of our lives have ashes and oil. When they come together through Easter, we are cleansed, saved, and sanctified.

When I am in need of a bit of holiness, I don't need Dr. Oz, nor do I need to *"laissez les bons temps rouler."* And as much as I think I need that sandy vacation, there might be another alternative. Instead, I just plan on getting a little soapy while I keep praying the alphabet.

TIE-DYE and TESTIMONY

TIE-DYE and TESTIMONY

This is what you shall do:
Love the earth and sun and the animals,
despise riches, give alms to every one that asks, stand up for
the stupid and crazy, devote your income and labor to others,
hate tyrants, argue not concerning God, have patience and
indulgence toward the people, take off your hat to nothing
known or unknown or to any man or number of men, go freely
with powerful uneducated persons and with the young and with
the mothers of families, read these leaves in the open air every
season of every year of your life, re-examine all you have been
told at school or church or in any book, dismiss whatever insults
your own soul, and your very flesh shall be a great poem.
—Walt Whitman, *Leaves of Grass*

There are way too many things to say about *T*.
First, let me get tuna fish out of the way. Eugene Peterson, in a writing workshop, told us that he constantly reminds himself that writing always comes down to tuna fish. He learned the hard way. In church newsletters, he would write the cover article expounding on a component of theology for the life of the church. At the end of the

newsletter, the church secretary would squeeze in a recipe for tuna fish casserole written by his wife. "All I would hear about," Eugene said, "was the tuna fish casserole."

I learned the hard way about tuna fish as well. I served tuna melts to my husband, Jason, on our first date. Years later, our kids still pray that Jason is the one with the apron on and pots in hand at six each night.

As I think about prayer, I wonder how the tangible informs the abstract: tuna fish casserole, theological insight. Tulips and truth. Tie-dye and testimony.

My daughter Leah suggests tacos for the letter *T*. "You can never have too many tacos," she tells me. Taco night at our dinner table usually means we are absolutely on the run, but resolute about our commitment to sit together, pray together, and talk together—no matter what. We hold hands, and in a ridiculously joyous prayer, wave the hands up and down while singing, "The Lord's been good to me and so I thank the Lord." *Thank*: now there is a T-word to talk about.

Eugene Peterson, Leah Hickman, and even Walt Whitman offer insight into *T*. "This," Whitman says. "This is what you shall do." I love how his words unfold into the testimony of a life well lived. "Do these things," Whitman says, "and your very flesh shall be a great poem."

Maybe the T-word that ties all this together is that "stand up, do something, and tell about it" word: *testimony*. In the tuna fish casserole recipe, there is a little testimony about busy households and the need to encourage one another. With the tacos, the salsa in the story is the testimony of a family together at the end of the day.

Sometimes we shy away from testimony. It feels self-righteous, or un-humble, or we worry we don't have a story to tell. But testimony is always about God, not about us. And our job is to simply, as best we can, talk about what God is up to in our crazy days.

Telling is the work of testimony. Maybe one of our problems with theology is that it can become, if we are not careful, too removed from the everyday. Maybe theology always has to have a little testimony—it has to bear witness to the Incarnation—that God is always in the flesh, never disembodied, always surprisingly graspable.

So I'm grateful for those moments when theology becomes testimony. Like Paul Tillich, one of the great theological thinkers of the twentieth century, who said about friend and mentor Elsa Brandström, "She made God transparent." That's what I'm talking about—testimony, that work of bringing in the real stuff of life by telling what saves us each day.

David Bailey wrote a great song about this kind of stuff, the testimony of words and pictures that embody hope and bear witness to the incarnate in the immediate. The words are deceptively simple, which usually is a clue that some well-thought-out testimony is about to be given. On a church retreat, his daughter Kelcey said, "I have a song I have to play for all of you." And then these words unfolded in the room:

Sunrise	*Blue sky*
Thin cloud	*Deep sigh*
Old road	*New day*
Left turn	*Right way*
Short path	*Long walk*

Big dreams	*Small talk*
Warm hand	*Cool breeze*
Short grass	*Tall trees*
Soft rain	*Hard night*
Red wine	*Moon light*
Slow song	*Quick dance*
First look	*Last chance*
Still sky	*Wild geese*
Sun set	*Great peace*
Two words	*To say*
To you	*Today*
Great	*peace.*

This is a song you have to listen to over and over again to get the deep sense of David's testimony. You see, David Bailey battled brain cancer for much of his adult life. He left the corporate world after receiving his diagnosis to pursue his passion for music. His singing changed the hearts and minds of many who were touched by his testimony, spoken with the accompaniment of a few strums on the strings of his guitar. David always wore two things: a bandanna, knotted around his head, and tie-dye.

When each day, each person, in one's life is precious, we understand the urgency, poignancy, and restraint of "two words, to say, to you, today." The extraneous is eliminated. The beautiful, paid attention to with astonishment and told about, urgently. I can't get enough of the song.

This is what you shall do. . . . And then your flesh shall become a great poem. So, here is the rest of the story. When David died, the hearts of many were broken. But David's family hoped otherwise. "Wear tie-dye," they told those who would attend his memorial service: "That is what David would have wanted."

So out came the RIT dye in every color imaginable. The middle schoolers at our church took on the task of creating shirts for everyone from our town who would make the six-hour journey to his home for the memorial service. We dyed tablecloths for the reception after the service. We dyed extra T-shirts for his daughter's sorority. You see, David had kids—teens and college students—and they needed his testimony to be visible. They needed that riotous burst of joy to be able to really remember their dad.

To be clear, someone had the bright idea of asking the wildly energized bodies of the tweens in our church to be turned loose with colors that stain permanently. So the church basement was pretty much tie-dyed as well that day: cement blocks, carpets, table, and, perhaps, even a stain on the ceiling. But it's tie-dye, and it bears a testimony of hope in hardship, so who can really complain about a smudge of cerulean blue, or outlandish yellow, or neon pink and green?

These are the kinds of stories I want to talk about over tacos (maybe not the tuna fish) at our table each night.

UNDERSTANDING and
UNDULATUS ASPERATUS
CLOUDS

UNDERSTANDING and UNDULATUS ASPERATUS CLOUDS

The most beautiful people we have known
are those who have known defeat,
known suffering, known struggle, known loss,
and have found their way out of the depths.
These persons have an appreciation, sensitivity, and an
understanding of life that fills them with compassion, gentleness,
and a deep loving concern.
Beautiful people do not just happen.
—Elisabeth Kübler-Ross

Beautiful people do not just happen. Elisabeth Kübler-Ross's line gives me pause as I continue my alphabetic prayers. What I love about her words as she talks about grief and defeat and struggle is the quest for *understanding* beneath these layers of loss and then, by some means of grace, a found sense of understanding. When I pray the alphabet, I am doing just that.

For nearly a decade I have prayed these words from

Isaiah upon each adult or child who joined the church:

> *The spirit of the LORD shall rest upon [him or her],*
> *the spirit of wisdom and understanding,*
> *the spirit of counsel and might,*
> *the spirit of knowledge and of the fear of the LORD.*

My hope is that these words will bolster and cloak the new member when necessary; so that in the depths, he or she will have sensitivity, compassion, and a deep concern; the capability to pray for a hard-won understanding.

This prayer for the gifts of the Holy Spirit, this prayer for a spirit of wisdom and understanding, was deemed so important by each congregation that they paused long enough to hear the undulating cadence of this text prayed for every person in the group to be welcomed, even if that necessitated twenty repetitions. Maybe the congregation's patience was a prayer in and of itself; they knew how much each young person would need the full strength of these words over the course of a lifetime. Knowing the unexpected ups and downs of their unfolding lives created a space for patience through the repetition. Every once in a while, I get an e-mail or a Facebook message from one of those candidates for confirmation saying something along the lines of "I am really struggling. . . . Help me understand."

The prayer for the gifts of the Holy Spirit follows that verse we so often hear during Advent: "A shoot will come up from the stump of Jesse; from his roots a Branch will bear fruit." Sometimes in the life of faith, we underestimate the number of stumps we will encounter. We need the reassurance of prayer and the encouragement of one another to look for the shoots of hope and the potential fruit. Is it possible that understanding and these other gifts all find their source in a stump, a dead and barren tree trunk?

The quest for understanding is something like the shape of a question mark, an undulating curve toward new knowledge, marked by a temporary pause upon arrival at an aha. All too often, that journey of understanding is the road of many questions, many curves, many pauses. Moments of insight followed by months of prayers.

Looking to understand is what turns our eyes to the clouds, to the heavens, to the presence of God that seems so remote in whatever situation we find ourselves. We look elsewhere, upward, outward. Will the clouds reveal a secret that we need in the now?

Paul Tillich understood life's quest in this way, that religion is a collection of ultimate questions and ultimate concerns. He offered in a moment of arrival: "Faith as ultimate concern is an act of the total personality. . . . Faith is the most centered act of the human mind. . . . It participates in the dynamics of personal life." I appreciate his use of the word *participates* because too often we want to turn away from the ultimate, the questions, a new understanding. We want the easy U-turn of returning to an easier past, rather than the not-so-certain present. But participation demands a sifting-through at the roots of the now to find a new understanding, a new way of being.

Maybe that's why we've all been downloading Zach Sobiech's song "Clouds," which begins with Zach playing the xylophone. Zach, a Minnesota high school senior, struggled against and then succumbed to cancer this year, but not without leaving all of us with a little bit of new understanding.

The lyrics tell the story of a young man who one day finds himself in a lonely hole, until he discovers someone sitting on the edge and holding a rope. He is invited to climb "up, up, up" to discover a new view. Once he reaches the clouds, he discovers there that the view is a little nicer. Six million views later, we've all been touched by Zach's understanding. He invited us to participate in the dynamics of his personal life, and to be changed in the struggle. While his family, I'm sure, prayed for a U-turn, he led many on the journey through the ultimate questions, singing and getting us all to look at clouds.

A few months ago, driving out Heather Heights near my house alongside the Amish farms, I looked up at the clouds and saw a cloud formation I had never seen before. The best way to describe these clouds is to say they were like the ribbon candy of childhood, undulating bands of water droplets and ice crystals. They were incredible.

Jane Wiggins first noticed this kind of cloud outside her office building in Cedar Rapids, Iowa, in 2009. Chad Hedstroom noticed them as well in Texas. Wiggins took a photo and sent it to the National Geographic Society and the Cloud Appreciation Society, who then classified this formation as undulatus asperatus.

Gavin Pretor-Pinney, cloud-lover and author of *The Cloud Collector's Handbook*, describes the undulatus asperatus cloud formation as the "Jacques Cousteau cloud," because when looked upon from below, it looks like the undulating ocean. The natural world, unfolding in these amazing new definitions, invites ongoing participation in new moments of understanding.

As we participate in the ultimate concerns of life, there are moments when we all—with Zach's encouragement—need to look up, up, up and with wonder and amazement realize that our feet may stumble over a few stumps, but with the help of that sevenfold gift of the Holy Spirit in wisdom and understanding, counsel and might, knowledge and fear, all held together by the spirit of the Lord, we are offered grace and invited to look up, down, and around in awe and wonder.

The importance of these gifts of the Holy Spirit is all too easy to forget, but Brian Shanley won't let us forget. He is unambiguous in his celebration of our need for this understanding in all the ups and downs of life:

> What the gifts do over and above the theological virtues is dispose the agent to the special promptings of the Holy Spirit in actively exercising the life of the virtues; the gifts are necessary for the perfect operations of the virtues, especially in the face of our human weakness and in difficult situations.

In those difficult situations, a shoot will come up, a rope will be let down, a cloud will catch our eye, and for a moment we will understand. That understanding will help us participate more fully in the richness and complexity of a life that undulates, but ultimately uplifts. Perhaps that is why the Ojibway Indians pray, *Sometimes I go about pitying myself and all the while I am being carried across the sky by beautiful clouds.*

VOTIVE SHIPS
and VOWS

VOTIVE SHIPS
and VOWS

O Lord of the oceans,
My little bark sails on a restless sea,
Grant that Jesus may sit at the helm and steer me safely;
Suffer no adverse currents to divert my heavenward course;
Let not my faith be wrecked amid storms and shoals;
Bring me to harbor with flying pennants,
hull unbreached, cargo unspoiled.
I ask great things,
expect great things,
shall receive great things.
I venture on Thee wholly, fully,
my wind, sunshine, anchor, defense.
The voyage is long, the waves high, the storms pitiless,
but my helm is held steady,
thy Word secures sage passage,
the grace wafts me onward,
my haven is guaranteed.
—Puritan prayer

Enter just about any church in Finland, and you will find a model ship gracing the ceiling and hovering over the center aisle of the sanctuary. These handmade offerings made in thanks for a safe return from a tumultuous trip on the sea are referred to as "votive ships."

When a seaman returned from a voyage, he crafted a model of the ship on which he had sailed and brought it to his church as an offering. It was a tangible expression of humility and thanksgiving; the ship a visible vow to live differently in response to being saved.

V is an up-and-down kind of letter. Can't you just see the peak and the swell of that stormy ocean wave as you look at its dip? Votive ships and those vows of thanksgiving offer a particular spiritual discipline even this far into the alphabet journey: *vow to build monuments of thanks*. In other words, let your very life be a thank offering.

During the season of Epiphany, the votive ship resonates with the hymn "I Saw Three Ships Come Sailing In"—a symbol of the wise men who journeyed to Jesus bearing thank offerings. This Finnish tradition also brings to mind the testimony of Psalm 107, particularly Eugene Peterson's translation. Verses 23-32 come as an answer to verse 2: "Let the redeemed of the LORD tell their story":

> *Out at sea you saw GOD in action,*
>   *saw his breathtaking ways with the ocean:*
> *With a word he called up the wind—*
>   *an ocean storm, towering waves!*
> *You shot high in the sky, then the bottom dropped out;*
>   *your hearts were stuck in your throats.*
> *You were spun like a top, you reeled like a drunk,*

> *you didn't know which end was up.*
> *Then you called out to GOD in your desperate condition.*

For us landlubbers, the tradition of offering votive ships—as it echoes Psalm 107—deepens our understanding of vocation. Out at sea, the sailor lived out a particular calling, a vocation to harness the wind, guide the sails, and deliver the goods, no matter the storm. But, when spun like a top out there at sea, the sailor questions the vocation and doesn't know what end is up. Certainly, we in our various vocations can relate to the sailor's desperate conditions. We set our eyes on the stars, choose a path, and chart a course. Then the bottom drops out. We are set adrift. What next?

For the sailor, the stress in that desperate condition makes him cry out to the Lord and make a vow of, well, whatever. *Get me out of this situation, God, and I will do whatever you ask of me.* That initial vow is easily said in the moment, because in that primal and gut-wrenching fear, the sailor would promise *anything*.

The votive ship takes that initial vow, made in that desperate moment, and lengthens the process of reflection. Once the vow is made, the storm survived, and the sailor back on dry land, it would be all too easy to ignore the promise and get back to living as one did prior to the storm. But the votive ship, and the process of building the ship slowly, piece by piece, invites a prayerful reflection over a prolonged period of time.

Picture the sailor home with family on a winter's night after a hearty dinner and conversation. Instead of returning to prior patterns, the sailor goes to the woodshop and pulls out the tools. The blueprint for the design is laid out on the desk, the balsa wood and fine tools by its side. Then, every cut and every measure becomes a focal point for prayer. *I survived. I must live differently.*

This new life becomes a prolonged vow as the sailor responds in gratitude to the act of being saved. The votive ship is a visible symbol of this invisible grace.

Votive ships are thank offerings that connect work and worship. The beauty of the votive ship is that it intimately connects the spheres of work and worship. The daily vocation of the sailor, in all of its peril and glory, is brought into the sanctuary. Too often we separate these spheres of life and create that impassable divide between Sunday and Monday. Gratitude for survival in the workplace, brought to expression in the sanctuary, bridges that divide and transforms the gratitude we offer in worship into the daily world of work.

Votive ships are physical expressions of God's invisible love and grace. While Psalm 107 creates within us a physical reaction of seasickness, the psalmist testifies to the invisible love and grace of God made manifest in breathtaking ways. If the call of stewardship is to consider how to make tangible the immense love and grace experienced in life's storms, then the next step of stewardship is to make that tangible expression accessible to a world of need. Perhaps stewardship is, at its best, really seawardship. These are vows, promises made, to respond to God's good actions through our changed lives.

After the offerings of the votive ships, the sailors eventually have to face seaward and venture back into the open sea that has proved tumultuous before. Maybe the life of faith carries that same current as well. We experience a desperate condition. We experience God's grace. We pause to tell the story. We create a physical expression of that thanksgiving. Our courage to testify emboldens others. But in the end, we go out once again into that vast sea to face life's challenges.

When I pray the alphabet and get to that downward arrow, that open cup of *V*, amazing things come to mind: velvet, violins, vibrancy, vines, and virtue. But I keep thinking about those votive ships hanging over my head when I walked through the sanctuaries of the churches in Finland. I keep thinking about the vows made in the craftsmanship of each ship. And I keep wondering, *What am I on the verge of creating? What will my votive ship be?*

Recently I heard of a young father, a graduate of a prestigious university with an MBA, who volunteers in a significant way at his son and daughter's elementary school. He lives in a small, depressed town in the Rust Belt when he would much rather be near the larger vistas for running, and the open roads for biking, that the Southwest offers. But here, where his wife landed a position as a professor, he lives into a particular vocation—one that is somehow an offering of thanks, a building of a boat, a lighting of a votive. His best intelligence, strength, and motivation are directed toward not just his children, but their peers, in a school that needs his greatest strengths. I'm not sure what seafaring journey led him to this place of being settled some place other than where he might have hoped, but I admire his offering.

Maybe he has internalized, more than I, this beautiful prayer from the Puritans written for sailors about to begin their voyage. This prayer of the Puritans helps even a land-lubber like me and so I pray:

> This day will bring me nearer home,
> Grant me holy consistency in every transaction,
> my peace flowing as a running tide,
> my righteousness as every chasing wave.
> Help me to live circumspectly,
> with skill to convert every care into prayer,
> Halo my path with gentleness and love,
> smooth every asperity of temper,
> let me not forget how easy it is to occasion grief;
> may I strive to bind up every wound,
> and pour oil on all troubled waters.
> May this world this day be happier and better because
> I live.
> Let my mast before me be the Saviour's cross,
> and every oncoming wave the fountain in his side.
> Help me, protect me in the moving sea until I reach the
> shore of unceasing praise.

WONDER and
WHEELCHAIRS

WONDER and WHEELCHAIRS

O Lord my God, when I in awesome wonder /
consider all the works thy hand hath made ...

On the news this morning, the photograph of a second-grade class in British Columbia created a stir. Miles Ambridge sits several feet at a distance from the rest of his class aligned on the requisite bleachers for a singular reason: his wheelchair.

I'm praying the alphabet, and I am definitely praying for Miles Ambridge, and now here at the letter *W* it would be tempting to go toward water lilies or watermelons, but I keep thinking about the strain in his neck to get closer to his class and that wheelchair, which provided both freedom and frustrating restraint.

A wheelchair demands respect, and so I have to pause here, to give proper thanks for the opportunity provided and the obvious need for deeper inclusion. Anyone who utilizes a wheelchair commands my respect as well: here, wisdom dwells because you can't navigate this world on wheels and not know a bit more than the rest of us about love and respect, openness and dignity. I'd like to talk to Miles. I'd love to hear his wisdom about this world. I'd love to know what he wonders about and what he wishes for.

A few years ago, I had a run-in with a wheelchair. Our confirmation class was sleeping over at a church in Pittsburgh. Leave it to a late-night game of hide-and-seek at that lock-in to provide an invitation for a few wheelies in the sanctuary's backup wheelchair. By midnight, one of the guys—a straitlaced, good-natured kid—said, "Lisa, I have a confession to make . . ." And sure enough, we had well-damaged that wheelchair. Everyone, myself included, felt absolutely terrible. Like I said, a wheelchair demands respect.

So the next morning, at a different church, we were absolutely dumbfounded when during the announcements a man from the church stood up to share about a fund-raiser he would be participating in: "I'm going to be pulling a wheelchair behind my bike for a hundred miles to promote awareness about disability." Our group sat stunned. Was this serendipity or, better yet, providence?

Quickly, the stunned glances turned to somewhat-loopy laughter. We had to giggle to let out the strange grace that was unfolding around us. Because we were at a very informal church, the pastor asked, "Would someone like to add a comment to that announcement?" And then our confession poured out.

After worship, we started talking about how God might use our neglect of that wheelchair toward the good. We brainstormed ideas and then came up with something as simple as this: we too would tow a few dilapidated wheel-chairs around our community on the back of our bikes. On the Sunday after the confirmation service, folks brought their bikes to do twelve laps in honor of 1 Corinthians 12:12: "Christ is just like the human body—a body is a unit and has many parts; and all the parts of the body are one body, even though there are many." We chose that passage humbly, recognizing our limitations as a community and how we needed to better understand and connect to all the varying abilities and bodies and gifts in our wider community.

We raised some money that day. We paid a little penance. We were blessed by a matching gift from a local bike company. We offered the money raised toward the medical mission partnership we have in the Dominican Republic so that someone in need, maybe even several in need, might receive the gift of a wheelchair, a gift of freedom.

It's funny that we consider the verb *wonder* and feel like it's a "passive, lay around and reflect" kind of spiritual discipline. Wonder is something you do on your feet, in the depths of life, as you puzzle and pray and strive for a better world. Those confirmation kids were *wondering* what a better life might look like for someone in need in the Dominican Republic.

Our kids learned that day they damaged the wheelchair, and so did I. We became a little wiser. But even more so, we were left with just a touch of wonder. Wisdom and wonder are two of the seven gifts of the Holy Spirit prayed for in the confirmation blessing. Wonder falls with awe under "fear of the Lord," which sounds imposing but is really an invitation to be involved in what God is up to in our world. Perhaps

162

there is a spiritual discipline as simple as this: *see a wheel-chair; pray for wonder.*

Nancy Eiesland, an amazing theologian, understood both the freedom and the limitations of a wheelchair. In her book *The Disabled God,* she struggled to come to terms with her own disability as a paraplegic and to make sense of who this God she loved was. I have no doubt that Nancy Eiesland *wondered* about a lot of things. But now, even after her death, she is renowned for her work in bringing to the forefront of America a better culture and wiser laws for those, like Miles, who live with a varying ability. But when first released, her work was cutting-edge, particularly in the incredibly unique way she came to picture God.

For Nancy, God resided in a sip-puff wheelchair, one that would be used by those who are quadriplegic. For her, this God was not omnipotent. Nor was this God a victim. Instead, God was a survivor, triumphant despite some debilitating limitations, victorious even when viewed by others as weak.

I want to talk to those confirmation kids about this picture of God. Could they imagine God in that wheelchair, the one used for wheelies during the lock-in? What would they wonder about this Lord God?

This is the kind of awesome wonder that propels poets, philosophers, and preachers and pushes us all to consider all of God's works. If we are going to comprehend anything, even the hardest things, our life work begins with a very active kind of wondering.

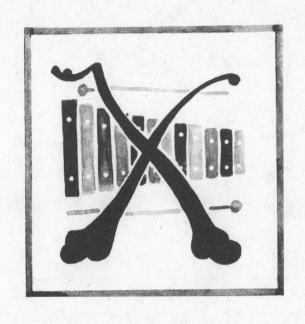

XYLOPHONES and EXILE

XYLOPHONES
and EXILE

X deserves more.
X is special, a symbol, shouting, Don't do it!
And kindly too, warning of dangerous crossings,
strange, dark roads travelled alone.
Mysterious, an unknown quantity—who really knows
what X represents? I wish I were prolific as X,
which goes forth and multiplies: 2x, 5x, 7x . . .
—Diane Lockward, "I'm Lonely as the Letter X"

On the news this morning was the photo of a young girl who is battling cystic fibrosis and waiting for a lung transplant. She was playing the xylophone in her hospital room while she waited.

While she fights cystic fibrosis, her parents are fighting the transplant system that allows adults with less pressing health concerns to have priority in organ donations. While Sarah is a top priority on the pediatric list, organ donations from children are rare. She is ten. To make the adult list, she must be twelve. Two years, in her condition, is way too long to wait. All she wants is to be well. "I want to be famous and be onstage and sing and dance, and play my xylophone," she says. But for now, you might say, she is in exile.

I can't stop thinking about her photograph—the sea of spaghetti tubes filling the hospital room, the cold angles of the machinery creating a harsh landscape, the gray elephant-trunk tube that delivers much-needed oxygen to her lungs. In the midst of this, her eyes focus on one thing: the mallet in her hand striking one of the rosewood bars on the scale. She is resolute. She will make music. The round mallet will hit the rosewood bar that presses against the underlying resonator. Even in exile, she will resound.

X is a hard letter. So bear with me as I push its boundaries just a bit. But X does provide an axis, a place from which to pause and look around a bit at what in our world deserves more. Certainly this little girl is on my alphabetic list. And when I consider what theological dictionary kind of word needs to come alongside that xylophone of hers, I know absolutely that it is *exile*.

Exile is that place where everything is wrong in life, even God. Exile is banishment, forced removal, a strange new place that has not been freely chosen. If you cross out *wrong* and write in the letter X, there's an acronym to easily re-member: Everything is X (wrong) In Life, Even God. Well, almost. Maybe the acronym doesn't work, but maybe that doesn't matter because you have been there and you know exactly what I am talking about.

Exile is the hospital room, the health condition, the failed marriage, the prodigal child. Exile is the lost job, the forced move, the misunderstood, the heavy weight. Exile is that unchosen circumstance that forces soul work, produces spiritual growth, and yet is battled every step of the way. Exile is suffering. In exile, all the other buffers in life are gone. There is you, the situation, and God. Which one will persevere?

Work with me here on the letter X, for truly we are at a crossroads in the alphabet. Are you an "X is half-full," or "X is half-empty" kind of person? Does X mean more, or absence? For those who say X is a wrong answer, a place of danger, a potential hazard, an ill-rated production, X is half-empty.

Ask anyone who has ever prayed the alphabet. Emma is my resident expert, and it is clear that X is a place of struggle. This is Jacob wrestling with God through the night—arms locked, chest-to-chest, who will prevail? The strain to find the name, the place, the thing that can be summed up by the letter X is difficult. Ask any Scrabble player, and it is quickly clear that X is very rarely a noun. X is much more a state of being: a difficult circumstance, a wrong, a danger, something that is no longer. Sometimes, though, X is a kiss.

For those who know X is a kiss, there is no better letter (remember those written sheets in envelopes?) than one signed with X's and O's, that is, kisses and hugs.

X is Xanadu, paradise, a place of possibility. X marks the spot and that is a good thing; there is buried treasure here, once we gain our senses, gather our tools, and dig in. X is that factor of exponential multiplication. X is more than half-full. X keeps on giving.

In the Hebrew Scriptures, that crossroads where X marked the spot, was the story of the exile of the Hebrew people who were taken forcibly to Babylon. Every prophet in the Old Testament is dated according to their chronological relationship to the exile. Are they a prophet of hope or doom, judgment or joy? The answer depends on the way they approach the seminal circumstance of the Exile. The psalmist spoke to the suffering when he wrote,

> Alongside Babylon's streams,
> there we sat down,
> crying because we remembered Zion.
> We hung our lyres up
> in the trees there
> because that's where our captors asked us to sing;
> our tormentors requested songs of joy:
> "Sing us a song about Zion!" they said.
> But how could we possibly sing
> the LORD's song on foreign soil?

The poetic irony of these words is that the psalmist's lament of not being able to sing actually *becomes* a song, even in exile.

"X deserves more," the poet wrote. So does God. When in exile, everything becomes wrong in life—even God; the hope of transformation, the hope of becoming relies on a person's ability to be changed. Exile makes us relate to God, self, and neighbor in new ways, ways previously unsung. How, in exile, may I be as prolific as *X*? Will I, like Sarah in her hospital room, be able to pull out my xylophone and start playing *X*'s song?

Perhaps our hope is in Christ, who, strangely, is sometimes known by the letter *X*. Think Xmas. While some lament that swiftly written shortcut, the Greek language tells a different story. The name of Christ is Χριστός which comes to us in English as "Christ." Look for Christ's name in any icon, and one might see the letter *X* marking his name. Our culture might tell us that *X* marks the spot, but sacred Scripture tells us that spot is always marked and met by Christ. Even exile.

When you are praying the letter *X*, the spiritual discipline needs to be just this: *Exclaim help for those who are lonely. Exclaim help for those who are in exile. Exclaim help for those who deserve more.* Then pray that they might find whatever kind of xylophone helps them sing, lament, and be heard in their exile.

YELLOW
and YAHWEH

YELLOW
and YAHWEH

*There are painters who transform the
sun to a yellow spot,
but there are others who, with the help of their art and their
intelligence,
transform a yellow spot into sun.*
—Pablo Picasso

When Caitlyn, our youngest, finally gave voice to words, we practiced labeling everything around us to increase her vocabulary. A typical conversation went something like this:

"Caitlyn, what color is Big Bird?"

"Red," she answered with definitiveness.

"No, Caitlyn. What color is Big Bird?" I asked while waving Big Bird before her eyes.

"Green."

"No, Caitlyn. What color is Big Bird?" My tone flattened with frustration.

"Blue."

Having proceeded through the whole of the color wheel, I sighed and said, "No, Caitlyn. Big Bird is yellow."

"Good job, Mom," Caitlyn said with encouragement and joy. "You got it!"

Yellow is always encouraging, even if it takes awhile to get the concept.

I'm thinking about yellow on the grayest of days. You might say I'm yearning for yellow. Yellow shouts with a robust and joyous list of all kinds of alphabet prayers:

Daylilies. Sunshine. Sunflowers. Lemons. Fall leaves. Grapefruit. Swallowtail butterflies. Canaries. Macaroni and cheese. Bananas. Baby chicks. Sweet corn. Taxicabs. Lance Armstrong's "Livestrong" bracelet to battle cancer. Buttered popcorn. The famed yellow submarine. No. 2 pencils. Highlighters. Golden retrievers. A daisy's center. I'll pass on the mustard.

As praying the alphabet today lands me on the letter *Y*, I know that life is wide open with this kind of letter. *Y* stands with its feet planted and arms raised to the sky, wide open in praise.

Luckily, yellow brightens *Y*. Today I'm grasping *Y*'s tail and holding it up like a cup to capture all that is joyous and sunny, even on this gray day. I'm praying, *Lord, fill my cup and let it overflow.*

Funny that the very name for God in the Old Testament had a "fill my cup" kind of quality. Yahweh, one of the several names for God in Scripture, was so holy that it was never uttered. One of the reasons it could never be uttered was that it comprised four letters—*Y-H-W-H*—without any vowels. Because it was missing those vowels, it could never be said correctly aloud. Because it was so holy, it was never spoken. When a rabbi came to those letters in Scripture, he said, "Adonai," instead of "Yahweh." What I love about that sense of deep respect is that it is an invitation for God to meet and fill and bless. God's very being is so big it overflows from any name that tries to contain it.

In a wonderful short story by Diane Glancy, Noe is a Mexican artist living in Brownsville, Texas. While he is sheltered in his small shed of a studio, other residents of the town are swept up in a joyous revival. Noe is not interested. God is too removed, too distant, too abstract for Noe. While he postures himself against this revival, one can't help but wonder if he's quietly praying for his own cup to be filled to overflowing.

Noe doesn't get God, but he is drawn to yellow. In his painting, he tries to "find the essence at the core of yellow." The land of Brownsville might be barren, burnt, and dry, but yellow electrified everything. His artwork revolved around capturing yellow.

When reading the story, you can't help but wonder if this Yahweh—the "I am what I am, I will be what I will be, and create what I will create" God—is revealing God's self to Noe in the vibrancy of yellow.

But still, God remains hidden to Noe.

The story paints a picture of him, "surrounded in his work shed with metal files, clamps, drills, sandpaper, turpentine, rags, small brushes with bristles hardened with dried paint . . . tubes of yellow paints, some of the letters covered with paint, which made the tubes read, *low, el,* and others simply, *yel*."

With just a few strokes, Glancy shows us that God is present but always hidden. We see glimmers, but the glimmer of God is always masked by bits of hardened paint.

As the story unfolds, we see that the Maker appears to Noe wearing a yellow poncho and commands Noe to build a church for the masses gathering in the revival. "I want you to paint it yellow," God says to Noe.

What if all churches were painted yellow? Goldenrod. Sunflower. Lemon yellow. Mellow yellow. Electrified yellow. Sunshine.

We would bring all our whys to the church and yield to that color yellow, the one Noe knew as the Maker. The one we know as Yahweh.

And there in the golden glow of the walls, we would worship and wail, pray and praise, sing and sit in silence. Yellow would fill our cups. Yellow would lift us up. We'd breathe yellow in and sigh gray out. Joy would radiate from the center of our golden circles. Justice and mercy, love and hope, humility and hope would flower.

Look at the painting by Paul Klee titled *Landscape and the Yellow Church Tower*, and you'll be instantly drawn in. Not because of riotous joy that can feel all too prickly if you are not in that place. Klee draws in the viewer to the tower of the yellow church by naming the grays, by etching some of those Y's into the lines of the painting. The dark corners and shadows catch our weary hands and draw us into that place of worship.

When God caught the hand of Moses, God led him through the gray and smoke of burning leaves toward the brilliant center of the burning bush. There, God revealed

God's very name to Moses—that mysterious and cryptic name that can never really be spoken aloud: Yahweh.

This name is so holy and precious, so difficult to get a handle on, so utterly unutterable that the Hebrew language omits the consonants. This name is unnameable. The four letters in English, *Y-H-W-H*, only hint at the weight and depth of the Hebrew letters known as the Tetragrammaton. The name might as well be a tube of paint with hardened crusts of yellow masking a letter here and a letter there. Yell. El. Ow.

God asks Moses to lead the people out of the shadows of oppression in Egypt into the light of the Promised Land. Along the way, a community will be formed. A community of worshipers. A community of yellow-lovers. They will live by certain commandments. They will wander in the wilderness. They will whine. But in the end, they will gather at the Tabernacle, that tent of meeting, and find even in the desert the golden shimmer of God.

Caitlyn struggled to name yellow. So do we.

Sometimes we *yell*.

Sometimes our *ow* gets the better of us.

Sometimes we are just too *low* to see.

Praying the alphabet allows us to see what Noe, in his art studio of a shed, struggled to understand. God appears in drips and splashes, not in grand and complete revelations. The living Lord is as present and viable and joyful as that tube of yellow paint on Noe's desk. This is true for our lives as well. But there is always just a little something veiling the divine. Moses wanted to see God face-to-face but had to settle all too often for the incomplete and partial. And even there, on that yellow paint covered with acrylic masking so many of the letters, are those letters *el*. El, another name for God. This Yahweh, the one who will be what he will be, cannot be covered up.

We pray the alphabet to scratch off some of the paint of our days and see what is underneath the veneer of what we all too often yawn at and take for granted. What we see underneath might echo the joy of this passage: "No matter how many promises God has made, they are 'Yes' in Christ. And so through him the 'Amen' is spoken by us to the glory of God."

And so every once in a while, no matter how bleak the corners of our lives are, we step into a sanctuary and see glimpses of that overflowing abundance of God. We hear an "Amen." We see a holy "Yes." The arc of a halo. The glimmer of a star. The play of light. The sheen on a Communion cup. For a moment, we pause. We yield. We give thanks for yellow.

And then Yahweh might just say to us, "Finally, you got it."

ZIN *and* ZINNIAS

ZIN and ZINNIAS

Scarcely a day of my life has gone by when I've not stirred the alphabetical ant nest, yet every time I type or pen the letter Z, I still feel a secret tingle, a tiny thrill.
—Tom Robbins

Praying the alphabet leads you down a long road toward *W*, *X*, *Y*, and *Z*. There we wander in the wilderness, explore those *X*'s of doubt and exile, yield with arms upheld to God in prayer, and finally zoom in on that odd letter *Z*.

Just a few questions have guided that journey. John O'Donohue invites us to answer: "From the evidence—why was I given this day?" This is a question someone who gives thanks for cottonwood trees and covenants can answer with blessed assurance. Anne Lamott hopes we will be transformed: "Have you become more generous, which is the ultimate healing? Or more patient, which is a close second? Did your world become bigger and juicier and more tender?" These are questions that someone who has held mercy in one hand and a melon in the other can answer wholeheartedly.

And this last question, asked by an organization that works with kids of varying abilities: "What did you do today that was amazing?" I love that the question leads us through the maze of our days from *A* to *Z* and asks us to be amazed, to stand in amazement, to give thanks for amazing grace. This is a question that, when answered by someone who knows the truth of both love and lemons, can be leaned into and produce a little praise.

What did you do today that was amazing?

Today I went up Heather Heights, about a mile from my house, where a line of Amish farms grace the rolling hills. There in the greenhouse Jason and I picked out flowers that could withstand our neglect and yet perk up a bit when met with a little water and our persistent smiles. We walked amid pansies and basil, geraniums and tomato plants, and then lingered by the gerbera daisies and the zinnias. They were all amazing.

Zinnias have not always been the most appreciated of flowers. When the Spanish first saw zinnias in Mexico, they deemed them *mal de ojos,* that is, "sickness of the eye." Zinnias may have experienced some disrespect, but today they are highly regarded among gardeners for their sturdiness, their diversity, and their great range of colors and design. When I look at a zinnia I see a sunburst—radiant and abundant petals bursting with light. Butterflies and hummingbirds love zinnias.

My final prayer here in these pages is for those zinnias, and for an odd landscape in Scripture: the Wilderness of Zin.

The Wilderness of Zin is one of those desert areas where

the Israelites wandered for forty years on their way to the Promised Land. If zinnias are bright and beautiful, the Wilderness of Zin is the opposite: barren and brutal to the one who travels through it. In our spiritual lives, I believe we are always somewhere back and forth between Zin and zinnias.

This final chapter is not about Zen. Nor zebras. And the Wilderness of Zin is nowhere close to holding a class of white zinfandel in your hand. There is not a paucity of Z's in the Bible: there is Zion, that biblical homeland so highly politicized now. And there is *zoe*, a great Greek word that illumines what eternal life in the here and now, today, might look like: on fire, alive, open, and pulsing with the very presence of God.

But I've picked the Wilderness of Zin because isn't life all about the wild places, those lost back roads, those dry and arid places where abundant life seems impossible to tap into? Resources are bare there and the rivers are dry. This is that place where we are looking for milk and honey but all we find is dirt and rocks.

I've thought about that kind of wilderness out in the desert of Arizona. The psalmist says, "I raise my eyes toward the mountains. Where will my help come from?" I realized one day that the psalmist looked to the mountains because the dirt at his feet was so barren, so impossibly unbeautiful. So darn ugly. Z is about that Wilderness of Zin, that barren place where we seek transformation and so we might, just might, start praying the alphabet to be lifted and changed.

Maybe that's why so many of us look to Cheryl Strayed and her book *Wild* as a modern-day Moses to lead us all through the wilderness of cancer, of addiction, of meaning-lessness, of necessary but seemingly impossible change. She leads us all on an exodus through circumstance. Can we be transformed in the wilderness?

Moses said to those on the journey with him,

> Go up there into the arid southern plain and into the mountains. You must inspect the land. What is it like? Are the people who live in it strong or weak, few or many? Is the land in which they live good or bad? Are the towns in which they live camps or fortresses? Is the land rich or poor? Are there trees in it or not? Be courageous and bring back the land's fruit.

His command necessitated courage. They ventured then into the Wilderness of Zin, arid and deserted. Later, with perseverance, they would discover pomegranates and figs. But at first glance, would it be possible for them to answer that question: *What did you see today that was amazing?*

You see, the ultimate fruit of faith is the ability to venture into the desert and draw forth water from the rock, manna from the most arid place, and then return to say, "This truly is amazing," instead of "What the heck is this?"

Two archaeologists, Leonard Woolley and T. E. Lawrence, ventured into the wilderness of Zin, only to echo the sentiment of Lawrence of Arabia:

> The wearing monotony of senseless rounded hills and unmeaning valleys makes this southern desert of Syria one of the most inhospitable of all deserts.

The Wilderness of Zin lies near the Scorpion Pass. One has only to whisper "scorpion," and I am flat on the ground in fear. In our anything but strenuous lives where we rely on certain creaturely comforts to encourage and persevere, can we find in our own wild places those amazing things, those words of praise?

Maybe that is where we rely on zinnias. Zinnias take us full circle from *A* to *Z*. They are from the family *Asteraceae,* but somehow they are known on the far end of the alphabet by the daily name: zinnia. How can these no-nonsense, practical flowers maintain such a joyous resolve to shout out with a riot of color? This is the kind of presence you need in the desert. In so doing, they attract butterflies and hummingbirds. Poet Valerie Worth offers this in praise of zinnia's amazing attributes:

> *I know*
> *Someone like zinnias; I wish*
> *I were like zinnias.*

Praying the alphabet is a spiritual discipline that hopes to attract butterflies and hummingbirds. When we become more like zinnias, stout and resolute, yet joyous in color and clout, anything is possible, even in that Wilderness of Zin.

When you begin praying the alphabet, it's funny how new things stand out and catch your attention. While praying about Zin and zinnias, I happened across an incredible quotation by Howard Zinn. Of course, that *Z* stood out in bold. And then, as I meditated on his message, I wondered if he might be like those zinnias and have a word for us as well:

184

To be hopeful in bad times is not being foolishly romantic. It is based on the fact that human history is a history not only of competition and cruelty but also of compassion, sacrifice, courage, kindness. What we choose to emphasize in this complex history will determine our lives. If we see only the worst, it destroys our capacity to do something. If we remember those times and places—and there are so many—where people have behaved magnificently, it energizes us to act, and raises at least the possibility of sending this spinning top of a world in a different direction. And if we do act, in however small a way, we don't have to wait for some grand utopian future. The future is an infinite succession of presents, and to live now as we think human beings should live, in defiance of all that is bad around us, is itself a marvelous victory.

Praying the alphabet is about that energy to act; it's about the possibility of spinning our complicated world in a creative new dimension. It is about acting in small ways, through an infinite succession of presents. Praying the alphabet is about behaving magnificently and mercifully, with the hope of victory through the God who is both Alpha and Omega, toward a new future where we zoom in on all that is good and right and just, and then give thanks for the amazing.

Conclusion:
Praying the Alphabet

I hope as you've been reading along that you have taken notes in the margins, making sure to remember the alphabet of your days. Or maybe you pulled out a theological dictionary to thumb through and discovered a new word or two. And perhaps you've discovered a new taste for Campbell's alphabet soup: just warm, stir, and spoon up a word for the day. Let that word become the topic of table conversation in your home. When you find P-O-R-C-H in your spoonful, what stories does that call forth in your family? When you see O-C-E-A-N, what memories can you share around the table?

There are many ways to pray the alphabet. What's most important is to remember those two hands of prayer: one hand on the ordinary stuff of your day-to-day, the other hand stretched toward the holy. Then, when you bring these two hands together in prayer—what conversation emerges?

ALLELUIA, AZALEAS.
BELIEF, BUMBLEBEES.

COMMUNION, CHOCOLATE.
DIVINE, DAFFODILS.

Epictetus, in his book *The Art of Living,* said, "Caretake this moment. Immerse yourself in its particulars." This is the starting point of praying the alphabet: to be a caretaker of the present moment by immersing yourself in its divine particulars. Name those particulars, and let their unique details draw you into a conversation with the divine presence made known to us in Jesus Christ.

So here are your ABCs, your beginning steps, for praying the alphabet:

> *A*ttend to the particulars of the day and name those incredible details.

> *B*e open to what God might be saying to you in their unique qualities.

> *C*onsider what theological words might have a conversation with what you named.

Let your creativity engage in joyous and raucous conversation with the divine presence in your life. Let new words emerge from the jumble of the day-to-day. This kind of prayer, like any prayer, takes work. This work is hard not because there is a right way and a wrong way. The work is hard, instead, because praying the alphabet is a habit of mind and heart that is first and foremost about attention. The problem is that so many *other* things call out for attention, and we let ourselves be lured by those evasions that take us away from the beauty of right here, right now.

Epictetus, who was a Greek sage and philosopher, continued,

> Quit the evasions.
> Stop giving yourself needless trouble.
> It is time to really live; to fully inhabit the situation
> you happen to be in now.
> You are not some disinterested bystander.
> Exert yourself.

This book is an invitation to become an interested bystander as you name the amazing things around you. This kind of prayer takes a bit of exertion. But the joy is found in the incredible conversation that emerges as you listen in— hearing mercy anew, tasting melons as if for the first time.

What emerges from this prayer is a new appreciation for the alphabet of the world around us, but even more so, what emerges are actions toward God and neighbor that are shaped by this new language. You'll find an ability to respond in new ways, as Epictetus says, "to this person, this challenge, this deed." This is what an alphabet of grace looks like: we respond with *mercy* to this person, we respond with *love* to this challenge, we respond with *imagination* to this deed because we have identified these qualities as we have prayed through our theological alphabet.

The sculptor Robert Indiana will forever be known for four letters he stacked together: *L-O-V-E*. The letter *O* he tilted to the right, just a smidge. Bystanders are drawn to this image simply because these four letters make them pay attention in a new way, almost as if that slight tilt of the *O* opens a new lens through which to see their ordinary world. Praying the alphabet is simply about calling those letters that we all too often take for granted to the forefront, so that we can see and appreciate their vivid reality in our lives. Then we see the world in a new way. We love in new ways. Robert Indiana's image is iconic for its simple invitation. What words will you call forth? What letter will you tilt, just a bit, and invite us to take a closer glance?

As you pray the alphabet, take notes. Begin to watch for what stands out in bold. See in those details opportunities to love and serve the Lord with gladness. Be gentle to yourself, giving time and space for a new discipline of praying to emerge. Epictetus concluded: "No great thing is created suddenly. There must be time. Give your best and always be kind."

This discipline of praying from *A* to *Z* will spark a sense of wonder, unearth new paths for joy, and kindle a little kindness as you live out what you learn in prayer.

Acknowledgments

Thank you to Don Ottenhoff of the Collegeville Institute's Ecclesial Literature Project and the summer writing workshops for providing the space to stumble into a new way of praying given time and creative space. Thank you to the banks of Stumpf Lake for the inspiration of "mercy and melons" with every muddy footstep while enjoying its beauty. Thank you to the team at Collegeville, including Carla Durand and Elisa Schneider. Thank you to Lauren Winner for hearing the idea and offering encouragement. Thank you to Lil Copan of Abingdon Press for saying yes.

Thank you to all whose stories are stewarded here. Thank you for your permission to tell them. May the letters of their telling come alive with new breath for all who read.

Thank you to Bill McCoy, who in his leadership at New Wilmington Presbyterian Church encouraged the session to pray through the alphabetic directory, naming each congregation member in prayer. Thank you to Sally Huey and the praying Sarahs—Norrie, Margaret, Ginny, Pat, Mary Louise, and Peggy—for continuing that tradition.

Thank you to the Writer's Almanac and its daily dose of poetry for offering inspiration to begin each day. Thank you to the artistic vision of Cleveland Clinic and the many artists represented there. Special thanks to Jaume Plensa and his two pieces there, *Cleveland Soul* and *Whispering*, for offering visual prayers. He said, "I always dreamed about transforming letters into something physical." Likewise, this book is my attempt to do just that—but to transform letters into a transformed life.

Thank you to the *Pittsburgh Post Gazette* and *Faith and Leadership* for permission to reprint excerpts from previous articles here. Thank you to the design, marketing, and publicity teams at Abingdon, including Sonua Bohannon, Julie Gwinn, Brenda Smotherman, Katherine Johnston, and Mary Johannes.

Thank you to a circle of friends: Sarah, Valerie, Mary, Jessica, Karen, Kim, Diana, Elaine, Arlene, Joyce, and Anne.

Love and thanks to Jason, Leah, and Caitlyn, who together help me enter into every letter with all my strength.

We learn the alphabet first in our family systems: for my family and extended family, thank you from *A* to *Z*, and back again.

Resources for Praying the Alphabet

Buechner, Frederick. *The Alphabet of Grace*. New York: HarperCollins, 1989.

———. *Beyond Words: Daily Readings in the ABC's of Faith*. New York: HarperCollins, 2004.

———. *Wishful Thinking: A Seeker's ABC*. Oxford: Mowbray, 1994.

Driscoll, Jeremy. *A Monk's Alphabet: Moments of Stillness in a Turning World*. Boston: New Seeds Books, 2006.

Kushner, Lawrence. *The Book of Letters: A Mystical Hebrew Alphabet*. New York: Harper and Row, 1975.

Munk, Michael L. *The Wisdom in the Hebrew Alphabet*. Brooklyn: Mesorah, 1983.

Norris, Kathleen. *Amazing Grace: A Vocabulary of Faith*. New York: Penguin, 1999.

Schulman, Grace. "God's Letters." In *Days of Wonder: New and Selected Poems*. New York: Houghton Mifflin, 2002.

Vandenberg, Katrina. *The Alphabet Not Unlike the World*. Minneapolis: Milkweed Editions, 2012.

Websites:

The Spirituality and Practice website and their alphabet of
spiritual literacy:
http://www.spiritualityandpractice.com/practices/
features.php?id=15309

Praying the names of God:
http://prayerleader.blogspot.com/2009/06/praying-abc-
names-of-god.html

Notes

book epigraph: Brian Doyle, *Leaping: Revelations and Epiphanies* (Chicago: Loyola Press, 2013), 27. When asked about the missing letter *w* Brian Doyle said, "as to why no *W*, I haven't the faintest, I say, grinning." I suppose one might say he is still praying the alphabet.

Introduction

epigraph: John O'Donohue, *To Bless the Space Between Us: A Book of Blessings* (New York: Random House, 2008), 98.
pg 11: Sculpture by Jaume Plensa, *Cleveland Soul,* 2007. Sculpture may be seen at http://my.clevelandclinic.org/arts_medicine/art-program/about-art-program.aspx.
pg 12: Arthur Green and Barry W. Holtz, *Your Word Is Fire: The Hasidic Masters on Contemplative Prayer* (New York: Schocken Books, 1987), 43.
pg 14: This story is attributed to Anthony de Mello, SJ.

A   ADVENT and AVOCADOS

epigraph: Seth L. Sanders, "What Was the Alphabet For? The Rise of Written Vernaculars and the Making of Israelite National Literature," *Maarav* 11, no. 1 (2004): 44.
pg 22: Ephesians 4:6.

B   BIRDS and BE

pg 24: Emphasis added: Psalm 46:10, NIV; Luke 1:38, NKJV; Leviticus 11:45.
pg 25: Psalm 104:1, 12.
pg 26: Matthew 6:26.
pg 28: Angela O'Donnell, "God's Sloth," *Bearings* 1, no. 1 (2009): 19. Used with permission.

C COVENANT and COTTONWOOD TREES

epigraph: Agbonkhianmeghe E. Orobator, "A Prayer for a Traveler," in
Theology Brewed in an African Pot (Maryknoll, NY: Orbis, 2008), xiii.
pg 32: Celia Brewer Marshall, *A Guide through the Old Testament* (Louisville, KY: Westminster/John Knox Press, 1989), 35.
pg 32: John 1:39.
pg 33: John 21:22.
pg 34: Genesis 9:15.

D DOWN COMFORTERS and DOUBT

epigraph: Rainer Maria Rilke, *Letters to a Young Poet,* translated by Joan
M. Burnham (Novato, CA: New World Library, 2000), 87.
pg 39: The St. Thomas Mass is held at the Mikael Agricola Church in
Helsinki, Finland. For more information see: http://www.tuomasmessu.
fi/lang/english/.
pg 41: John 20:28.
pg 41: Rilke, *Letters to a Young Poet.*

E EVERGREENS and ETERNAL LIFE

epigraph: John Bartlett, *Bartlett's Familiar Quotations,* ed. Justin Kaplan
(Boston: Little, Brown, 2002), 122:26.
pg 47: John 20:31.

F FROGS and FUTILITY

epigraph: Ecclesiastes 1:2, Holman Christian Standard Bible.
pg 50: Ecclesiastes 1:2.

G GRASSHOPPERS and GLORY

epigraph: Walt Whitman, preface to *Leaves of Grass: 1855 First Edition Text*
(Radnor, VA: Wilder, 2008), 11.
pg 56: Mary Oliver, "The Summer Day," in *The Truro Bear and Other
Adventures: Poems and Essays* (Boston: Beacon, 2008).
pg 56: Job 38:36-37.
pg 58: Charles Wesley, "Love Divine, All Loves, Excelling," in *The United
Methodist Hymnal* (Nashville: Abingdon, 1989), 384.

H HARMONY and HONEY

epigraph: Sue Monk Kidd, *Secret Life of Bees* (New York: Penguin Books,
2002), 84.
pg 63–64: Genesis 43:11; Exodus 3:17; John 3:4; Proverbs 25:27.
pg 66: Romans 8:28.

I IMAGINATION and ICICLES

epigraph: This quote is attributed to Albert Einstein.

pg 70: I'm grateful to Stephanie Paulsell for this phrase. See http://www.ptsem.edu/lectures/?action=tei&id=youth-2005-03 for her essay "With Energy, Intelligence, Imagination and Love: Leadership in Youth Ministry" from The 2005 Princeton Lectures on Youth, Church, and Culture.

pg 71: Book of Order: Presbyterian Church (U.S.A.) (Louisville, KY: Office of the General Assembly, 2011/2013), 123. See Directory for Worship W-4.4003h.

J JUSTICE and JELL-O

epigraph: Harper Lee, *To Kill a Mockingbird* (New York: HarperCollins, 1988), 124.

pg 76–77: Kathy Stephenson, "Jell-O Haiku Contest: Invasion of Gelatinous Gems from Readers," *Salt Lake Tribune,* November 20, 2012.

pg 77: Tom Andrews, ed., *On William Stafford: The Worth of Local Things* (Ann Arbor: University of Michigan Press, 1995), 110.

pg 78: Nori Huntsman, in Stephenson, "Jell-O Haiku Contest."

pg 78: See Micah 6:8.

pg 79: Susan Sandretto, Keith Ballard, Pam Burke, Ruth Kane, Catherine Lang, Pamela Schon, and Barbara Whyte, "Nailing Jello to the Wall: Articulating Conceptualizations of Social Justice," *Teachers and Teaching* 13, no. 3 (2007): 307–22.

K KIMONOS and KINGDOM

epigraph: Leslie Esther, *Walter Benjamin: Critical Lives* (London: Reacktion Books, 2007), 169.

pg 86: 2 Corinthians 5:17.

L LOVE and LEMONS

epigraph: Academy of Achievement: A Museum of Living History. Accessed May 17, 2004: http://www.achievement.org/autodoc/steps/pas?target=jon1-005.

pg 90: 1 Corinthians 13:4.

pg 90–92: Anne Morrow Lindbergh, *Locked Rooms and Open Doors: Diaries and Letters of Anne Morrow Lindbergh, 1933–1935* (New York: Harcourt Brace Jovanovich, 1974), 231.

pg 92: Hosea 14:4.

M MERCY and MELONS

epigraph: Alonzo Mansfield Bullock, *Lincoln* (Appleton, WI: Appleton & Lange, 1913), 155.

pg 95: John Albrecht Bengel, *Gnomon of the New Testament* (Edinburgh, Scotland: T. & T. Clark, 1915), 156.

pg 96: Anne Lamott, *Help, Thanks, Wow: The Three Essential Prayers* (New York: Penguin, 2012), 21.

pg 96: Matthew 5:7.

pg 97: This verse is widely connected to Jesus' teaching on the Sabbath, particularly in Mark 2 and Matthew 12. See for example: William Buck Dana, *A Day for Rest and Worship: Its Origin, Development and Present Day Meaning* (New York: Fleming H. Revell Company, 1911), 263.

pg 98: KYRIE. Words and Music by Richard Page, Steve George and John Lang. © 1985 WB MUSIC CORP., INDOLENT SLOTH MUSIC, PANOLA PARK MUSIC and ALI-AJA MUSIC. All Rights Administered by WB MUSIC CORP. All rights reserved. Used by Permission of ALFRED MUSIC. Secured March 25, 2014.

N NAUTILUS and NOT YET

epigraph: From Jennifer L. Holm, *The Trouble with May Amelia* (New York: Simon and Schuster, 2011), opening quote.

pg 102: Christopher L. Heuertz, *Unexpected Gifts: Discovering the Way of Community* (New York: Simon and Schuster, 2013).

pg 103: Samuel McChord Crothers, *Oliver Wendell Holmes: The Autocrat and His Fellow-Boarders* (New York: Houghton Mifflin, 1909), 64.

O ORIGAMI and OVERCOME

epigraph: From the film *Between the Folds,* written and directed by Vanessa Gould. Demaine, featured in the film, is the youngest professor ever hired by M.I.T., a MacArthur "genius" Award winner, and an origamist.

pg 106: John 16:33, NIV.

pg 108: Romans 5:2-5.

pg 110: Kylie Morris, "Thais Drop Origami 'Peace Bombs," BBC News, December 5, 2004, http://news.bbc.co.uk/2/hi/asia-pacific/4069471.stm.

P PRAYER and the PHOSPHORESCENT BAY

epigraph: George Herbert, *The English Poems of George Herbert* (London: Longmans, 1902), 47.

pg 113: John M. Buchanan, "Testing God: Prayer Works for Those Who Pray," *Christian Century* 123, no. 9 (May 2, 2006): 5.

pg 113: Walter A. Brueggemann, Letter to the Editors, *Christian Century* 123, no. 14 (July 11, 2006): 44.

Q QUESTIONS and QUEEN ANNE'S LACE

epigraph: Rupert Shortt, *Rowan Williams: An Introduction* (London: Darton, Longman & Todd, Ltd., 2003), 3.

pg 119: See the blog: http://www.googlepoetics.com. Curated by Sampsa Nuotio.

pg 120: Mark 9:24, NKJV.

pg 120–21: Northumbria Community, http://www.northumbriacommunity.org/who-we-are/the-rule-deeper.

pg 121: Job 38:4-5.

pg 122: Ronald A. Bosco and Joel Myerson, *The Later Lectures of Ralph Waldo Emerson, 1843–1871,* vol. 2 (Athens: University of George Press, 2001), 321.

pg 122: Kathleen Norris, *The Quotidian Mysteries: Laundry, Liturgy and "Women's Work"* (New York: Penguin, 1998).

R RAINBOWS and RESURRECTION

epigraph: David L. Larsen, *The Company of the Creative: A Christian Reader's Guide to Great Literature and Its Themes* (Grand Rapids, MI: Kregel, 1999), 210.

pg 128: Colossians 3:12-14.

S SOAP and SANCTIFICATION

epigraph: Karen Weekes, ed., *Women Know Everything!: 3,241 Quips, Quotes, and Brilliant Remarks* (San Francisco: Chronicle Books, 2007), 417.

T TIE-DYE and TESTIMONY

epigraph: Walt Whitman, *Leaves of Grass: 1855 First Edition Text* (Radnor, VA: Wilder, 2008), 9–10.

pg 142: Paul Tillich, *The New Being* (New York: Scribner, 1955), 28.

pg 142–43: Used with permission from Leslie Bailey. © David M. Bailey. See: www.davidmbailey.com. From album, "Coffee with the Angels," available at: http://www.cdbaby.com/cd/dmbailey02.

U UNDERSTANDING and UNDULATUS ASPERATUS CLOUDS

epigraph: Elisabeth Kübler-Ross, *Death: The Final Stage of Growth* (New York: Simon & Schuster, Inc., 1975), 96.

pg 147: Isaiah 11:2, KJV.

pg 147: Isaiah 11:1, NIV.

pg 148: Paul Tillich, *Dynamics of Faith* (New York: HarperCollins, 1957), 4–5.

pg 149: See: Michael J. Crumb, "Iowa woman's photo sparks push for new cloud type" on *The Missourian* (June 21, 2009). Accessed May 2, 2014: http://www.columbiamissourian.com/a/115080/iowa-womans-photo-sparks-push-for-new-cloud-type/. See also: "Asperatus Cloud, Iowa," National Geographic, http://news.nationalgeographic.com/news/2009/06/photo
galleries/new-cloud-pictures/.

pg 149–50: Gavin Pretor-Pinney, *The Cloud Collector's Handbook* (San Francisco: Chronicle, 2011).

pg 150: "Asperatus Cloud, Iowa," *National Geographic*.

pg 150: Brian Shanley, "Review of *Knowledge and Faith in Thomas Aquinas by John I. Jenkins*," *Thomist* 63 (1999): 318.

V   VOTIVE SHIPS and VOWS

epigraph: Stephen Fortosis, ed., *A Treasury of Prayers: A Collection of Classical and Modern Expressions of Faith* (Grand Rapids, MI: Kregel Publications, 2001), 62.

pg 153: Psalm 107:2, NIV.

pg 153–54: Psalm 107:2, 23-32, The Message.

pg 156: Fortosis, ed., *A Treasury of Prayers,* 62.

W   WONDER and WHEELCHAIRS

epigraph: Lyrics to "How Great Thou Art," words by Stuart K. Hine.

pg 160: Rebecca Klein, "Miles Ambridge, 7-Year-Old In Wheelchair, Isolated By Photographer In Class Picture" in *The Huffington Post* (June 17, 2013). Accessed online May 3, 2014: http://www.huffingtonpost.com/2013/06/17/miles-ambridge-wheelchair-class-photo_n_3454857.html.

pg 163: Nancy L. Eiesland, *The Disabled God: Toward a Liberatory Theology of Disability* (Nashville: Abingdon, 1994).

X   XYLOPHONES and EXILE

epigraph: Diane Lockward, "I'm Lonely as the Letter X," in *Eve's Red Dress* (Nicholasville, KY: Wind Publications, 2003), 14.

pg 169: Psalm 137:1-4.

Y   YELLOW and YAHWEH

epigraph: Quote widely attributed to Pablo Picasso.

pg 174: Diane Glancy, "The Man Who Said Yellow," *Image* 51 (2006): 7–13.

pg 177: 2 Corinthians 1:20, NIV.

Z ZIN and ZINNIAS

epigraph: Tom Robbins, *Wild Ducks Flying Backward: The Short Writings of Tom Robbins* (New York: Random House, 2005), 225.

pg 180: John O'Donohue, *To Bless the Space Between Us: A Book of Blessings* (New York: Random House, 2008), 98.

pg 180: Anne Lamott, *Help, Thanks, Wow: The Three Essential Prayers* (New York: Penguin, 2012), 21.

pg 181: The Children's Institute of Pittsburgh. See: http://www.amazing kids.org.

pg 182: Psalm 121:1.

pg 182–83: Cheryl Strayed, *Wild: From Lost to Found on the Pacific Crest Trail* (New York: Random House, 2012).

pg 183: Numbers 13:17-20.

pg 183: Lawrence James, *The Golden Warrior: The Life and Legend of Lawrence of Arabia* (New York: Skyhorse Publishing, 2014), 79.

pg 184: Valerie Worth, "Zinnias," *All the Small Poems and Fourteen More* (New York: Farrar, Straus and Giroux Books for Young Readers, 1994), 5.

pg 184–85: Howard Zinn, *A Power Governments Cannot Suppress* (San Francisco: City Lights Books, 2007), 270.

Conclusion

pg 188: Epictetus, *Art of Living: The Classical Manual on Virtue, Happiness, and Effectiveness,* edited by Sharon Lebell (New York: HarperOne, 2007), 113.

pg 189: Ibid.

Enjoy the New Companion Book with Spiritual Practices for Each of the 26 Letters of the Alphabet.

AVOCADO and ADVENT

BIRDS and BE

COVENANT and COTTONWOOD TREES

DOWN COMFORTERS AND DOUBT

EVERGREENS and ETERNITY

FROGS AND FUTILITY

GRASSHOPPERS and GLORY

[third image second row]

HARMONY and HONEY

[fourth image second row]

IMAGINATION and ICICLES

[fifth image second row]

JUSTICE and JELLO

26 Ways to Pray the Alphabet

A Companion Guide to Mercy & Melons | $9.99

Trade Paper 9781630888732; ePub 9781630888749

KIMONOS and KINGDOM

LOVE and LEMONS

MERCY and MELONS

NAUTILUS and NOT YET

ORIGAMI and OVERCOME

PRAISE and the PHOSPHORESCENT BAY

QUESTIONS and QUEEN ANNE'S LACE

RAINBOWS and RESURRECTION

SOAP and SANCTIFICATION

TIE DYE and TESTIMONY

UNDERSTANDING and UNDULATUS APERATUS CLOUDS

VOTIVE SHIPS and VOWS

WHEELCHAIRS and WONDER

XYLOPHONES and EXILE

YELLOW and YAHWEH

ZIN and ZINNIAS

Coming October 2014

Available online and wherever fine books are sold.

AbingdonPress.com

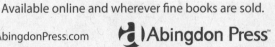

Abingdon Press™

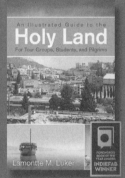